THE LIAHONA PRINCIPLE

THE LIAHONA PRINCIPLE

By Bradley R. Wilde

CFI
Springville, Utah

ISBN 13: 978-1-55517-932-0
ISBN 10: 1-55517-932-0

Published by CFI, an imprint of Cedar Fort, Inc., 925 N. Main, Springville, UT, 84663
Distributed by Cedar Fort, Inc. www.cedarfort.com

LIBRARY OF CONGRESS CATALOGING-IN-PUBLICATION DATA

Wilde, Bradley R.
  The Liahona principle / by R. Bradley Wilde.
    p. cm.
  ISBN 1-55517-932-0
  1. Church of Jesus Christ of Latter-day Saints. 2. Mormon Church. 3. Lehi (Book of
    Mormon figure) I. Title.

  BX8635.3.W54 2006
  289.3'32--dc22

                          2006022802

Cover design by Nicole Williams
Cover design © 2006 by Lyle Mortimer
Printed in the United States of America

10   9   8   7   6   5   4   3   2   1

Printed on acid-free paper

DEDICATION

To the members of the Worland Wyoming Stake, from whom I have learned the universal power and effectiveness of the Liahona Principle.

TABLE OF CONTENTS

1. From the Wilderness to Bountiful................ 1

2. The Most Correct Book.................................. 9

3. Where Am I? What Do I Do? 13

4. Mary Poppins and the Book of Mormon ... 19

5. The Three Ways... 25

6. The Easy Way 37

7. How to Use Your Liahona 45

8. Fourfold Responsibility 55

9. Responsibility to Family and Friends 59

10. Responsibility to Employer/Education 71

11. Responsibility to Church 85

12. Responsibility to Self 97

13. A Life-Changing Principle 115

About the Author 119

Chapter 1
FROM THE WILDERNESS TO BOUNTIFUL

Several years ago, we had an apple miracle. It occurred at a financially difficult time in our lives, and began when I read the following in the Book of Mormon:

> And it came to pass that we did again take our journey in the wilderness; and we did travel nearly eastward from that time forth. And we did travel and wade through much affliction in the wilderness; and our women did bear children in the wilderness.

> And so great were the blessings of the Lord upon us, that while we did live upon raw meat in the wilderness, our women did give plenty of suck for their children, and were strong, yea, even like unto the men; and they began to bear their journeyings without murmurings.
>
> And thus we see that the commandments of God must be fulfilled. And if it so be that the children of men keep the commandments of God he doth nourish them, and strengthen them, and provide means whereby they can accomplish the thing which he has commanded them; wherefore, he did provide means for us while we did sojourn in the wilderness.
>
> And we did sojourn for the space of many years, yea, even eight years in the wilderness.
>
> And we did come to the land which we called Bountiful, because of its much fruit and also wild honey; and all these things were prepared of the Lord that we might not perish. And we beheld the sea, which we called Irreantum, which, being interpreted, is many waters. (1 Nephi 17:1–5)

After reading those verses, I turned to my wife, Debi, and said, "That sounds like us!"

Like Nephi, we felt we too were in a wilderness, though ours was financial. Like the women in Lehi's family, my wife had also borne children in this wilderness. She too was strong and never murmured on our journey. Figuratively, we had lived off "raw meat," and like Nephi, we also knew that God had strengthened us and provided means for our support many, many times. As it was with this Book of Mormon family, amazingly enough, our wilderness journey had also been ongoing for eight years.

I said to Debi, "If these verses literally apply to us like it seems they do, then our eight-year journey is at an end, and the next place we come to is the land of Bountiful, with its much fruit and wild honey. Won't that be wonderful?"

That was the beginning of what we call our Miracle of the Apples.

A month after reading these verses, Debi was driving downtown when she saw a truck with Washington apples parked on the side of the road. We normally bought twenty or so boxes of apples to put in our root cellar for the winter but we had not yet done so this year. She stopped but was disappointed when she found the man selling the apples was asking $20 for a thirty-pound box. She told him we were interested but not at that price. Two days later, the weather turned cold, and it started snowing. That evening, the apple sales-man came knocking at our door. He was as surprised to see Debi as she was to see him. Monte said he had 150 boxes of apples that were going to freeze that night, so he was trying to sell them door to door. Debi told him that we could put them in our root cellar, and maybe sell them for him, if he would sell them for $10 a box; he agreed.

Monte explained that a couple of weeks earlier, he and a buddy had decided on a whim to go gleaning apples. They ended up pick-ing six thousand pounds of apples. They borrowed a friend's truck and brought them to Worland to sell. Monte did not give us the impression that he was spiritually oriented or that he was a hard worker, but he said that someone was sure watching out for them. He noted that they felt led to pick apples and that it was a last-minute decision. He said also that he felt watched over to find Debi a second time. We certainly agreed—we live a mile out of town and are not in any kind of neighborhood where you might go door-to-door selling. Regardless, Monte certainly recognized that they would have lost forty-five hundred pounds of apples had Debi not offered to take them.

We recognized that we too had been blessed. Here we were, with six children, without our winter store of apples. It was an awe-some and humbling realization to think that the Lord arranged to provide apples for us all the way from Washington, a thousand miles away, by inspiring two men we had never seen before.

Nephi said that they called the land Bountiful because of its much fruit and wild honey. We now had two and half tons of apples in our root cellar. We had never had so much fruit before—more than we could ever use for ourselves. So we were doubly blessed because we could share this miracle with others.

So we had the fruit mentioned in the scriptures, but what

about the honey? Debi always cooked with honey but our supply of honey was extremely low. The beekeeper from whom we bought our honey lived at the end of our street. When he asked if we needed more honey, we told him that we didn't have the money at the time. He brought several buckets to us anyway and told us to pay for it when we could. We knew the obtaining of the apples and honey was a very real miracle for us and a fulfillment of the impression we had received when reading 1 Nephi 17. We had literally arrived in our land of Bountiful.

That experience of finding ourselves in a Book of Mormon story, and seeing its literal fulfillment, opened our eyes to the power of the personal application of the scriptures. Since then, we have recognized ourselves hundreds of times in these sacred volumes. What we read inspires us, directs us, enlightens us, guides us, and gives us understanding of where we are in our life's journey. The power of opening the scriptures and finding ourselves has brought new meaning to Nephi's exhortation to "liken all scriptures unto us, that it might be for our profit and learning" (1 Nephi 19:23). We have come to learn that all of our problems are answered in the scriptures. In fact, it seems that the scriptures are like our own personal journal or handbook, prewritten and given to us as a companion to help us on our journey. All we have to do is open them to learn how best to proceed.

We have had broken bow experiences, found ourselves in "prison," walked the path of Laman and Lemuel, and been Abinadi, Alma, Ammon, the brother of Jared, Joseph Smith, Abraham, and so many others. Each time we have opened the scriptures, peace, enlightenment, and understanding have come, as well as some of most powerful insights into our own souls that we have ever received.

One morning I was meeting with all the zone leaders in the mission. As I was pondering what I might say to them, I randomly opened my scriptures, looking for a possible idea to share. I turned to Alma 37:39, a verse about the Liahona, the director or compass given to Lehi to guide his family in their journey. I read, "It was prepared to show unto our fathers the course which they should travel in the wilderness."

Wouldn't it be a great thing if missionaries had an actual Liahona to show them what they should do, the course they should travel in their missionary work? I thought. As I read further, it occurred to me that they literally do.

In Alma 37, Alma is passing on to his son Helaman several sacred things, including the Liahona, which he had received from Mosiah (see Mosiah 28:20). Alma tells Helaman that the Liahona is a type and shadow—meaning a model or representation—of spiritual things. Note what those spiritual things are and how they can guide us, just as the Liahona guided Lehi's family.

> And now, my son, I would that ye should understand that these things are not without a shadow; for as our fathers were slothful to give heed to this compass (now these things were temporal) they did not prosper; even so it is with things which are spiritual.
>
> For behold, it is as easy to give heed to the word of Christ, which will point to you a straight course to eternal bliss, as it was for our fathers to give heed to this compass, which would point unto them a straight course to the promised land.
>
> And now I say, is there not a type in this thing? For just as surely as this director did bring our fathers, by following its course, to the promised land, shall the words of Christ, if we follow their course, carry us beyond this vale of sorrow into a far better land of promise. (Alma 37:43–45)

Alma taught that the words of Christ are our Liahona. Those words can come from many places, but it is logical that the scriptures, the Book of Mormon in particular, would be our main source. Alma then counsels his son, "O my son, do not let us be slothful because of the easiness of the way; for so was it with our fathers; for so was it prepared for them, that if they would look they might live; even so it is with us. The way is prepared, and if we will look we may live forever" (Alma 37:46).

How often do we look? How often do we use our Liahona, our scriptures, our words of Christ? Are we slothful? Do we fail to look as often as we should because of the easiness of the way?

Are we missing out on some of the help and direction we could be receiving?

Elder Neal A. Maxwell counseled, "Brothers and sisters, on very thin pages, thick with meaning, are some almost hidden scriptures. Hence we are urged to search, feast, and ponder. Especially, however, we should also do more of what Nephi did, namely 'liken all scriptures unto [ourselves]'" ("Lessons from Laman and Lemuel," *Ensign*, November 1999, 6).

Elder Maxwell reaffirms the concept that there are scriptures, even almost hidden scriptures, that are personally applicable that we need to search out and liken to ourselves. We need to make better use of our Liahona.

Some time after this meeting with the zone leaders, I was attending a district meeting with six missionaries. Each companionship discussed an investigator they were working with who was having difficulty progressing, and then each taught principles from the discussions. When it was my turn, I taught what I call "the Liahona Principle."

First, I asked the elders that if they literally had Lehi's Liahona, would it give them insight about what to do with their investigators? They thought it might. We then discussed ways the Liahona enlightened Lehi's family and how the words of Christ, or the scriptures, might do the same for us—or even their investigators.

The purpose of this book is to encourage you, the reader, to open your Liahona, or the scriptures, to find the answers you are looking for. It doesn't matter what your questions are or where you open. Just open your scriptures, put yourself in them, and you will find the answers and direction you seek.

As a counselor in a stake presidency, as a stake president, as a counselor in a mission presidency, and as a bishop, I have seen the scriptures used this way thousands of times. In fact, when I give counsel in an interview, I often hand the person a copy of the Book of Mormon and say, "Let's see what the scriptures tell you." To the humble seeker of truth, an answer is always there; I've gained a deep testimony of that.

You are about to read about the experiences of many people who have opened the scriptures and found themselves described therein. Peace and direction have come to these individuals as Heavenly Father has spoken to them through His written word. He spoke to these people, and He will speak to you! I hope these stories will inspire and encourage you to look in your Liahona and find the answers Heavenly Father would give you about where you are in your life. He is more than eager to speak to all of us, and His written word is where His voice is most often and most clearly heard.

I appreciate the many people who shared their stories. For privacy reasons, their names are not mentioned in the book; names have been changed. However, all have given me permission to include their experiences. What a blessing to review so many wonderful stories and see how the scriptures have blessed so many lives.

I testify that your Liahona—the scriptures—will speak to you. Try using them right now! Think about where you are in life, what your major challenges are, what you are struggling with, or even what you should teach next in family home evening. Then open up the scriptures—it doesn't matter where—and put yourself into the verses you read. Apply the principles and teachings to yourself and to your question. If you receive the perfect insight right now, wonderful! But if you don't, mark the spot; we'll come back to it. At that point, you'll find it more meaningful to you, and you'll see more clearly how the scripture applies.

Chapter 2
THE MOST CORRECT BOOK

Most members of The Church of Jesus Christ of Latter-day Saints are familiar with the oft-quoted statement by the Prophet Joseph Smith, "I told the brethren that the Book of Mormon was the most correct of any book on earth, and the keystone of our religion, and a man would get nearer to God by abiding by its precepts, than by any other book" (Introduction, Book of Mormon). If that is the case, the Book of Mormon is the scriptural book to which we should most often turn for direction and enlightenment.

However, "*all* scripture is given by inspiration of God, and is profitable for doctrine, for reproof, for correction, for instruction in righteousness" (2 Timothy 3:16; emphasis added). We are also instructed to "feast upon the words of Christ; for behold, the words of Christ will tell you *all* things what ye should do" (2 Nephi 32:3; emphasis added).

✶

When I first became active in the Church I would go to each meeting very happy and excited. Then the music would begin. . . then a prayer. . . then the lesson, and soon I would be crying. Not just a tear or two but outright sobbing. Many people came up to me and asked if someone had died or if I had family problems I would like to talk about, but that was not my problem. No one had died, and my husband is the greatest support I could ever ask to have. So why was I crying? It was the mention of my Savior Jesus Christ. Just the mention of His sacred name made me cry. It reached the point where I thought I was going crazy or something. I remember trying to control this feeling. Nothing worked. I was just a big baby.

Then one day, out of the blue, the scripture James 1:5 came to mind: "If any of you lack wisdom, let him ask of God, that giveth to all men liberally, and upbraideth not; and it shall be given him."

For a minute or two I thought it was odd for me to go to the Lord and ask why I cried every time I heard His name mentioned but I knew I needed help! I knew I needed to follow the direction of James. As I knelt on the floor that Sunday afternoon, I was given an answer. I was told to study my scriptures, so that I might better know my brother Jesus Christ. I was promised I would understand the purpose for His life on earth. I was promised that if I read and studied about him, I would surely understand the meaning of His birth clear to the time He died for me.

That has been more than twelve years, now, and I am still learning about my Savior every time I open the scriptures. I still cry tears of sorrow and joy for Him. I know He knows me and who and what I am. Knowing this has made me a much better person. I am so thankful I have had the opportunity to get to know Him in such a wonderful, personal way.

So, though the Book of Mormon is the book that draws us nearer to God than any other book, the words of God also come to us in the Old Testament, the New Testament, the Doctrine and Covenants, and the Pearl of Great Price, as well as through the counsel of modern prophets.

Elder Boyd K. Packer taught:

> When I understood that the Holy Ghost could communicate through our feelings, I understood why the words of Christ, whether from the New Testament or the Book of Mormon or the other scriptures, carried such a good feeling. In time, I found that the scriptures had answers to things I needed to know.
>
> I read, "Now these are the words, and ye may liken them unto you and unto all men" (2 Nephi 11:8). I took that to mean that the scriptures are likened to me personally, and that is true of everyone else. . . .
>
> I learned that anyone, anywhere, could read in the Book of Mormon and receive inspiration. Some insights came after reading a second, even a third time and seemed to be "likened" to what I faced in everyday life.[1]

Elder Packer mentioned one of those insights:

> When I was 18 years old, I was inducted into the military. While I had no reason to wonder about it before, I became very concerned if it was right for me to go to war. In time, I found my answer in the Book of Mormon:
>
> "They [the Nephites] were not fighting for monarchy nor power but they were fighting for their homes and their liberties, their wives and their children, and their all, yea, for their rites of worship and their church.
>
> "And they were doing that which they felt was the

duty which they owed to their God; for the Lord had said unto them, and also unto their fathers, that: Inasmuch as ye are not guilty of the first offense, neither the second, ye shall not suffer yourselves to be slain by the hands of your enemies.

"And again, the Lord has said that: Ye shall defend your families even unto bloodshed. Therefore for this cause were the Nephites contending with the Lamanites, to defend themselves, and their families, and their lands, their country, and their rights, and their religion" (Alma 43:45–47).

Knowing this, I could serve willingly and with honor.[2]

Elder Packer then counsels, "When you feel weak, discouraged, depressed, or afraid, open the Book of Mormon and read. Do not let too much time pass before reading a verse, a thought, or a chapter."[3]

That counsel, when followed, allows us to see the hand of God in our lives. To encourage you to open your personal Liahona, and do it often, is the purpose of this book.

Notes

1. Boyd K. Packer, "The Book of Mormon: Another Testament of Jesus Christ—Plain and Precious Things," *Ensign*, May 2005, 7.
2. Ibid.
3. Ibid. 7–8.

Chapter 3

WHERE AM I?
WHAT DO I DO?

When the boy Joseph read James 1:5, he commented, "Never did any passage of scripture come with more power to the heart of man than this did at this time to mine. It seemed to enter with great force into every feeling of my heart" (Joseph Smith–History 1:12).

Why did this verse in James strike Joseph so deeply? Why did it have such a powerful effect upon him?

The religious revival going on during this time had Joseph

very confused. He wanted to join a church, but the confusion and strife among the different denominations were so great, he didn't know which one to join. He wondered which of all the denominations was right, and which were wrong. His words indicate that the confusion caused more than mere curiosity or wondering. Indeed, it created deep turmoil within his soul. It is enlightening to read what Joseph wrote and enjoy a glimpse into what he was thinking. His words are brief but profoundly revealing: "During this time of great excitement my mind was called up to serious reflection and great uneasiness. . . . My feelings were deep and often poignant. . . . My mind at times was greatly excited. . . . I often said to myself: What is to be done? Who of all these parties are right; or, are they all wrong together? If any one of them be right, which is it, and how shall I know it?" (Joseph Smith–History 1:8–10.) Reread and ponder those words, and you will gain a better feeling of Joseph's struggle.

During this intense mental and emotional turmoil, Joseph opened his Bible and read, "If any of you lack wisdom" (James 1:5). Imagine how he felt when he read those six words? We can almost hear him shout, "That's me! That is how I feel! That is where I am at! I lack wisdom! That is my problem!" Here he was, in a state of great confusion and uncertainty, and now he had read something that he could identify with. He lacked wisdom! Finally, something pinpointing his problem. No wonder he wrote, "I reflected on it again and again, knowing that if any person needed wisdom from God, I did; for how to act I did not know, and unless I could get more wisdom than I then had, I would never know" (Joseph Smith–History 1:12).

We can certainly understand Joseph's feelings. Where am I at? Where do I stand? Am I on the right path or not? These are questions we all ask, and we ask them often. Elder Boyd K. Packer, for instance, wanted to know if it was right for him to go to war. The verses he read in Alma calmed his mind and allowed him to "serve willingly and with honor."[1]

But Joseph's knowing where he was at was not enough. Another question had to be answered: What do I do? "For how to act," Joseph wrote, "I did not know" (Joseph Smith–History 1:12). He needed to know what the Lord would have him do. The next five words he read in James must have struck him like a lightening bolt. "Let him ask of God" (James 1:5). Again we can almost hear him shout, "That's it! That's what I have to do! I have to ask God!"

But knowing what to do doesn't necessarily make doing it easy. Apparently Joseph felt this prayer needed to be voiced aloud, something he had never done before and something he wanted to think through (Joseph Smith–History 1:14). "At length," he states, "I came to the conclusion that I must either remain in darkness and confusion, or else I must do as James directs, that is, ask of God. I at length [again after time had passed] came to the determination to 'ask of God,' concluding that if he gave wisdom to them that lacked wisdom, and would give liberally, and not upbraid, I might venture" (Joseph Smith–History 1:13).

You know the rest of the story. Joseph Smith acted on the scriptural instruction he was given, and his life changed. Though his life became immensely more difficult, he knew where he was at and what he needed to do. His soul was at peace. He would return to this pattern often throughout the rest of his life.

When Joseph opened the scriptures and found himself in James, it must have been a great relief to him. His deeply troubling questions regarding what he should do were answered. We can feel that same comfort and direction.

I had just been called to serve as a stake missionary. The call meant a release from another calling that I had loved and enjoyed. No one knew of my calling, as I had not yet been sustained.

In Sunday School, as I was contemplating this new calling and lamenting the release from my previous calling, the teacher asked us to open to one of our favorite scriptures. My scriptures fell open to Doctrine and Covenants 31:2, a verse I loved because it had come as an answer before, and probably because I had been back to read it so many times. But this time I felt compelled to read further into verse 3, which reads,

"Lift up your heart and rejoice, for the hour of your mission is come; and your tongue shall be loosed, and you shall declare glad tidings of great joy unto this generation."

I felt this scripture was given to me at this particular time to let me know that it truly was my time to serve as a stake missionary. It also showed me that the Lord would help and guide me and it would be a time of rejoicing for me. It turned out to be just that—a time of rejoicing! I loved that calling!

However, not all direction from the scriptures is so comforting. Sometimes, we may be even more confused when we open the scriptures and apply them to ourselves, or we may even be told things we don't want to hear. If we are patient and keep searching, enlightenment will come.

One summer I was feeling particularly down. I just didn't feel the joy that I used to. I had happy moments, but I wasn't really filled with joy. I spoke to my priesthood leader about it, and he recommended that I open the Book of Mormon and look for my answer there.

At home I prayed about what the problem could be and then randomly opened the Book of Mormon and began reading. "Repent," it said. Isn't that what half of the Book of Mormon says? I wasn't sure how to apply that to my life. I was going to church. I paid my tithing. I obeyed the Word of Wisdom and attended the temple. I just didn't know what I was supposed to repent of. So I tried again. I opened the Book of Mormon and read, "Repent." It was so frustrating! Over the next few days I tried this process several times with the same results.

Finally, I met with my priesthood leader again and told him of my experience. I told him I didn't know what it was that I needed to repent of. He told me to ponder on that and then open the scriptures. When I tried this, I began reading about pride. It wasn't like I thought I was better than everyone else. I truly tried to love and serve my fellow man. My leader counseled me on what pride meant and gave me a copy of a talk by President Ezra Taft Benson.

At home as I read and pondered this talk, I realized my problem. A new bishop had been called in our ward, and I was having a hard time accepting the way he did things. I was critical and judgmental. He did not do things the way I felt they should be done! Pride!

As I repented and changed my attitude, the joy that I desired so much came back into my life.

Where am I at? What do I do? This good sister found the answers to those pleas by opening her scriptures. She learned that pride was causing her depression and that repentance was her solution. Her Liahona taught her what she needed to know.

Notes

1. Boyd K. Packer, "The Book of Mormon: Another Testament of Jesus Christ—Plain and Precious Things," *Ensign*, May 2005, 7.

Chapter 4

MARY POPPINS AND THE BOOK OF MORMON

As I child, I loved the movie *Mary Poppins*. In that movie, Jane and Michael get a new nanny—Mary Poppins. When she moves in, she has only one bag, but when she unpacks, she pulls all kinds of things out of that single bag—a fancy hat to wear, a mirror for the wall, even a tall, tall lamp. Jane and Michael are amazed, and when Mary Poppins turns away for a minute they peek into the bag and under the table, trying to figure out how she does it!

Finally, Michael says to Jane, "That's tricky!"

Jane replies, "No, that's wonderful!"

The Book of Mormon is a little like Mary Poppins's bag. When we open the book and reach inside, we find many wonderful things that give answers to any situation we face in life. It is not tricky—it is wonderful! As Elder Boyd K. Packer says, "The Book of Mormon is an endless treasure of wisdom, and inspiration, of counsel and correction."[1]

A member of my stake shared the Mary Poppins/Book of Mormon analogy in a sacrament meeting talk. I was impressed by it and would further extend that analogy to all scripture, with a reminder that the Book of Mormon is the most correct of all books and the book we should most often turn to.

Elder Henry B. Eyring gave some valuable counsel and insight on personal revelation through scripture study. Note in particular how he goes to the scriptures with a question in mind.

> Throughout my life, the scriptures have been a way for God to reveal things to me that are personal and helpful. . . .
>
> The scriptures were one of the ways God spoke to me—even when I was a child—about my needs, my situation, and my life. They still are. Since our needs change over a lifetime, God has different things to tell us at different times.
>
> Sometimes I go to the scriptures for doctrine. Sometimes I go to the scriptures for instruction. I go with a question, and the question usually is "What would God have me do?" or "What would God have me feel?" Invariably I find new ideas and thoughts I have never had before, and I receive inspiration and instruction and answers to my questions. . . .
>
> Another reason to study it regularly, for me at least, is that I can pick up the Book of Mormon, open to any page, read, and the Holy Ghost bears personal witness to me that it is the word of God. I know the Lord is speaking. I know the Book of Mormon is what it claims to be. . . .
>
> Going to the scriptures to learn what to do makes all the difference. The Lord can teach us. When we come to a crisis in our life, such as losing a child or

spouse, we should go looking in the scriptures for specific help. We will find answers in the scriptures. The Lord seemed to anticipate all of our problems and all of our needs, and He put help in the scriptures for us—if only we seek it.[2]

Elder Eyring tells us that the scriptures should speak to us and give us personal instruction. We can even approach the scriptures with questions, such as "what should I do?" or "what should I feel?" and receive answers. We know that is what Joseph Smith did. Like Mary Poppins's bag, the answers are in there, just waiting to be pulled out.

✳

I just wasn't sure what I was supposed to do. Did the Lord really want me to serve a mission? Did I really want to serve a mission?

I had received my call to serve in an eastern states mission but was that where the Lord really wanted me to go? I didn't know anything about that area, and found it kind of hard to be excited about going there. Was I worthy and ready to serve a mission?

Here I was, traveling with my parents to go to the temple for my very first time, in preparation for my mission, and these were the thoughts running through my mind. I had been taught that when I have questions that need answering, or when I need counsel, I should open the scriptures and learn the Lord's will. I was taught that the scriptures I turn to will always be my answer, whether I understand it or not. The key is to find out *how* the scriptures apply in my life, rather than *if* they apply.

I certainly had questions running through my mind that morning, and I wanted answers. As we drove, I prayed for answers, then opened up my triple combination. Though I meant to open up to the Book of Mormon, I turned instead to the Doctrine and Covenants.

I had especially wondered if it was the Lord's will for me to serve a mission, and if the mission I was called to was really where He wanted me to go. The Lord knew the questions in my heart and provided answers in a way that most definitely eased my worries. I opened up to Doctrine and Covenants 66, and my eyes were drawn to verse 5: "Behold, verily I say unto you, that it is my will that you should proclaim my gospel from land to land, and from city to city, yea, in those regions round about where it has not been proclaimed."

In the words of Joseph Smith, "Never did any passage of scripture come with more power to the heart of man than this did at this time to mine" (Joseph Smith-History 1:12). I knew the Lord's will was for me to proclaim His gospel! I said a silent prayer, thanking God for my answer.

As I turned to look back at the scriptures, my eyes fell to verse 7, where I read, "Go unto the eastern lands, bear testimony in every place, unto every people and in their synagogues, reasoning with the people."

The Lord answered my second question! He didn't want me to go just anywhere but he had called me to serve out east. He knew where I was needed and had directed me there.

What gratitude I felt for the answers contained in the scriptures! I continued to read the entire section of the Doctrine and Covenants and found that the whole selection was meant for me. Almost each verse had special personal meaning to me! Though I was reading about blessings promised to someone else 170 years ago, the Spirit whispered to me that these were blessings the Lord was promising to me also.

As I served my mission, Doctrine and Covenants Section 66 was a special strength to me—a constant reminder of the Lord's will regarding me and the blessings I could receive. This strength came in recognizing that this was the Lord's way of speaking to me. This experience of opening the scriptures has occurred over and over again, each time with the same results. Though the answers have not always been so direct and powerful, they have always come.

And they will always come! In the words of Jane, "They are wonderful!"

Notes

1. Boyd K. Packer, "The Book of Mormon: Another Testament of Jesus Christ—Plain and Precious Things," *Ensign*, May 2005, 9.

2. Henry B. Eyring, "A Discussion on Scripture Study," *Ensign*, July 2005, 22–24.

Chapter 5

THE THREE WAYS

During a district meeting with a group of missionaries, I asked a question: If you had access to Lehi's Liahona, do you think it could give you insight into your investigators and how to help them? Of course, the missionaries agreed that it probably could. We then discussed three ways the Liahona helped Lehi's family and how the words of Christ, or the scriptures, might do the same for us—or our investigators.

1. THE LIAHONA GAVE LEHI'S
FAMILY DIRECTION

Nephi says this about the Liahona: "Within the ball were two spindles; and the one pointed the way whither we should go in the wilderness" (1 Nephi 16:10).

We are often looking for direction in our lives. What a wonderful thing to have books of scripture to point us in the direction we should go.

In January 2005, Joni was trying to make a decision about what she should do for the upcoming semester. She had just completed the first semester of her freshman year in college. She did not have the finances to return and had not filled out the necessary paperwork to apply for Federal Student Aid.

Since it did not look like she could return to school, she decided to move to a bigger city, get an apartment, and work. But a part of her really wanted to return to college.

One day, she decided to try finding an answer in the Book of Mormon. First she prayed and told Heavenly Father that she was going to move. Then she opened her scriptures and read. She came to me and said, "The Book of Mormon didn't give me any direction at all." I asked her what she had found, and she read it to me. I noticed right away that everything in that particular scripture was negative. It was dark, bad, depressing. I mentioned that to her, and then she could see it too.

We talked a bit, and she decided to try it again. This time, when she prayed, she expressed her desire to return to college for the second semester and said that's what she planned to do if she could get a confirmation. Then she opened her scriptures again. This time everything in the scripture was good and light and happiness. It was a complete opposite from the first scripture she had found.

That was all she needed. She came back to me and said she knew she was supposed to return to school. I helped her with the paperwork, we got everything worked out, and she completed the second semester of college.

It was her first experience finding answers in the scriptures. It really made an impression on her.

Joni learned she really did have a Liahona to direct her, and it literally showed her the course she should travel in her wilderness.

2. THE LIAHONA GAVE LEHI'S FAMILY UNDERSTANDING CONCERNING THE WAYS OF THE LORD

Not only were there two spindles in the Liahona, with one pointing the direction to go, but writing also appeared on the instrument, giving the family insight and understanding.

> And it came to pass that I, Nephi, beheld the pointers which were in the ball, that they did work according to the faith and diligence and heed which we did give unto them.
>
> And there was also written upon them a new writing, which was plain to be read, which did give us understanding concerning the ways of the Lord; and it was written and changed from time to time, according to the faith and diligence which we gave unto it. And thus we see that by small means the Lord can bring about great things." (1 Nephi 16:28–29)

How often do we desire understanding concerning the ways of the Lord? What a tremendous blessing to have the words of Christ to enlighten us and give us understanding of where we are at, or why things are the way they are, or what we should do. With faith, diligence, and obedience, those words change from time to time, according to our circumstances

To put it simply, my husband is an alcoholic. What I have endured because of this simple fact is not simple at all—many years of heartache, worry, fear, and disappointment—many hopeless days followed by many sleepless nights—unending pleas to heaven from the bended knee of a woman with a broken heart. Sometimes my heart was so heavy with grief it was as if my husband had died. I often felt like I was truly mourning his loss.

Logic told me that this was indeed a hopeless situation, that he was a lost cause. Sometimes I believed it. But always there was a feeling in me that there was more to be found than the logical. I felt there was something that the world didn't know, something completely illogical perhaps, but something real nonetheless, something that even I didn't fully understand.

Some of those around me felt that I should give up. They thought that I was enabling him in his addiction, and even causing more harm. Was I being stubborn or foolish? Was there anyone to turn to for direction? I felt completely alone in this situation. One particularly painful day, as I was facing the prospect of yet another sleepless night, I asked myself, "Am I wrong to hold on?"

I opened my Book of Mormon in a desperate search for an answer. I opened to Alma 19, and I received not only an answer but also a revelation. In Alma 19, King Lamoni was struck dumb and thought to be dead. The queen was told he was dead, but she called upon Ammon for help. "Go in and see my husband . . . some say that he is not dead, but others say that he is dead and that he stinketh, and he ought to be placed in the sepulcher; but as for myself, to me he doth not stink" (Alma 19:5).

Certainly there were those who thought my husband was hopeless and that I should "bury" him because he "stinks." I wept as I read. Could there be any scripture applied more literally to me at that moment? "He is not dead . . . therefore bury him not" (Alma 19:8). Heavenly Father did not want me to "bury" my husband!

Ammon asked the queen if she believed him, and she did, although she had no reason to believe other than his word. It was like the "something" that I couldn't see, or name, or logically believe, and yet I did. Ammon told the queen to watch over King Lamoni. The queen had faith that her husband would be spared; therefore she watched over him, and he did rise.

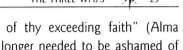

"Blessed art thou because of thy exceeding faith" (Alma 19:10). I suddenly felt like I no longer needed to be ashamed of my faith, or to be scared of having it. I truly felt that not only was I not foolish to have faith, but that I would be blessed for it.

King Lamoni and the queen went on to testify to the crowds and convert their people. I felt inspired that because of our troubles, our testimonies could touch other people's hearts and help them in their lives. I received revelation that we would be missionaries someday.

I knew that Heavenly Father was speaking to me. He knows me. He knew what that something was that I couldn't understand and that the world could not see. It was all right for me to see my husband differently than the world sees him. I knew that Heavenly Father wasn't going to leave me alone to grieve. Most important of all, I knew that when I needed answers, the answers could be found if I would just open my scriptures.

What a great blessing for this sister to open her Liahona and find understanding concerning the ways of the Lord. Her problem didn't go away, but with the added enlightenment, she was at peace and able to deal better with her situation.

3. THE LIAHONA HELPED LEHI'S FAMILY SOLVE PROBLEMS

Lehi's family had no food and suffered much. By following the directions from the Liahona, Nephi obtained sustenance for his family. "I, Nephi, did go forth up into the top of the mountain, according to the directions which were given upon the ball. And it came to pass that I did slay wild beasts, insomuch that I did obtain food for our families" (1 Nephi 16:30–31).

As we face problems, how wonderful to have the word of God to look to, to help solve those problems.

During that district meeting, my counsel to the missionaries who had investigators who were not progressing was to check with their other companion, the Liahona. Where? It didn't matter. They just needed to open their scriptures and read a verse or two and see what they could learn. I had them open their scriptures right then, and each companionship gained an important insight into an investigator they were concerned about.

When missionaries apply the Liahona principle, they can gain two great insights into how to help investigators. First, they can learn the true motivation of the investigator—where his heart really is. Second, they can learn what to teach, what the investigator needs to hear that will answer the questions of his heart.

✦

Ruth was one of our favorite investigators. She seemed to love the missionaries, the Church, everything. Yet she wouldn't attend meetings and wouldn't get baptized. The only television she watched was the BYU channel, and she had many LDS books she enjoyed. She had been baptized into the religion her family had belonged to for generations and could see no reason to change. What seemed to matter to her was to be a good Christian and to be good to your neighbor. We had worked with her for a long time to help her understand the importance of the gospel but couldn't seem to make any progress. We were stuck.

When we decided to try the Liahona Principle, my companion actually opened to the Topical Guide. We first thought maybe we should try again but then noticed that he had turned to the word "Christian." So we turned to the first reference listed, Acts 11:26, and there read, "And it came to pass, that a whole year they assembled themselves with the church, and taught much people. And the disciples were called Christians first in Antioch."

What a great scripture to share with Ruth! Wouldn't it be important for her as a Christian to assemble with the Church? Here was an idea we could build on to encourage her to attend meetings and to help further her progression in the gospel.

The Liahona Principle is an easy principle. Like Lehi, all we have to do is open our Liahona and look. For Lehi and his family, the writing on the Liahona changed from time to time, according to the faith and diligence they gave to it. So it is with us. If we need direction, if we are seeking to understand the ways of the Lord, if we have a problem that needs to be solved, then one of the first things we should do is open the scriptures and apply what we read to our situations. Most of the time, an answer will be waiting for us. As we apply and follow that answer with the requisite faith and diligence, we will see God's hand in our lives, and know that it is by Him that we are being led (see 1 Nephi 17:13).

Elder Dallin H. Oaks quotes Elder Bruce R. McConkie as saying, "I sometimes think that one of the best-kept secrets of the kingdom is that the scriptures open the door to the receipt of revelation."[1] The secret to opening the revelation door, then, would be opening the scriptures. However, because that seems so easy, we sometimes are slothful (see Alma 37:46) and forget to turn to these sacred records.

Elder McConkie continues, "All of us are entitled to the spirit of prophecy and of revelation in our lives, both for our personal affairs and in our ministry. The prayerful study and pondering of the holy scriptures will do as much, or more than any other single thing, to bring that spirit, the spirit of prophecy and the spirit of revelation, into our lives."[2]

We all want the spirit of prophecy and the spirit of revelation. We all want direction, understanding, and divine help in solving our problems. But how to go about receiving these often seems elusive or difficult. How do we prayerfully study and ponder? Where do we start?

Regarding the scriptures as a Liahona makes that process much easier, much more of a reality. Like Lehi, we need only to open our Liahona and look. Whether we read during daily scheduled study or randomly open the book, we will find answers. And pondering on what we find allows us access to that revelation talked about by Elder McConkie.

I was raised in a wonderful family with goodly parents who loved the Lord. They taught us the gospel in word and worked very hard to live it as well. Their testimonies were so strong, in fact, that they carried me into my thirties. Using the scriptures was something that I tried to do. I tried hard to read them with my children. I read the words for myself and for lessons for Church callings. But I didn't understand how to find answers that could help me on a daily basis with my problems of today.

I wanted to do more than read the words, I wanted to ponder and have the scriptures come alive. Then guidance came. I remember listening to my priesthood leaders speak and teach from the scriptures. The scripture stories they related were powerful and exciting. I found myself visualizing the people and their circumstances in my mind. Those priesthood leaders taught that I, as an individual, could gain answers to personal questions simply by contemplation of a question and then randomly opening the scriptures, and reading what was before me. It sounded simple—a little too simple to be true. However, I trusted my leaders and wanted to put them to the test. I was intrigued to see if Heavenly Father would guide me in that way as well.

I began using this method of learning when I had a question or was confused about something. I was actually shocked to find words on the page I turned to that had meaning and direct correlation to my question or thought. Time after time, I let the scriptures fall open and gained insight. Sometimes it would come in the first verse that my eyes fell on. Other times I read multiple verses, even pages. Every time I tried it, I was just as surprised as the first time that it worked for me.

I had always known that I should study the scriptures but it was very overwhelming and confusing to me to know what exactly to study. The "fall open" method had worked so well with random questions I had, I decided to see if it would help in scripture study. I let the scriptures fall open, then I read the chapter and looked up

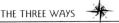

the footnotes that went along with the verses.

Once I became more comfortable with the content of the scriptures and learned that there were indeed messages directly for me, I gained understanding and confidence that I could read and ponder entire books of scripture. I felt I could be successful beginning a section within any of the larger books of scripture and then reading and pondering it.

I now love the scriptures. I can now say for myself that I know they are true. I know that the answers to my problems and the direction for my life can be found in the scriptures. I can feel the power of God speaking to me and testifying that Jesus Christ is His son and that He lives. I now have the peace that comes with knowing how much They love me.

I was recently called to be the gospel doctrine teacher. Even though the thought of teaching adults is overwhelming, studying the scriptures in preparation is not. In fact, it is the best part of my day.

As we apply the Liahona Principle, we must remember that the Liahona was not the only source of spiritual enlightenment available to Lehi and his family. They had the brass plates, prayer, dreams, visions, angels, the gift of the Holy Ghost, a prophet/father's counsel, and father's blessings. Inspiration might also have come through hymns, counsel from parents and spouses, Sunday School-type lessons, and so forth.

So it is with us. We have many sources of inspiration and direction available. Church leaders, prayer, dreams, visions, angels, blessings, hymns, mothers, fathers, children, classes, the Holy Ghost, books, and magazines are a few sources of the words of Christ. We can't do without them. But our Liahona, the compass that gives us the most direction, understanding, and help, has to be the scriptures. This must be why we are counseled to study the scriptures daily.

If our Liahona is so valuable, why don't we make better use of it? Alma counsels, "For behold, it is as easy to give heed to the word of Christ . . . as it was for our fathers to give heed to this compass" (Alma 37:44). We would be wise to follow Alma's counsel and give heed to this compass we have been given. It is easy. All we have to do is look. As Elder Henry B. Eyring said, "Going to the scriptures to learn what to do makes all the difference."[3]

Does it matter which book of scripture we turn to? As stated previously, because of its purity and status as the most correct book on earth, the Book of Mormon is the Liahona we should most often turn to. President Ezra Taft Benson gave this strong directive: "At present, the Book of Mormon is studied in our Sunday School and seminary classes every fourth year. This four-year pattern, however, must not be followed by Church members in their personal and family study. We need to read daily from the pages of the book that will get a man 'nearer to God by abiding by its precepts, than by any other book.'"[4]

President Benson then issued several challenges, including the following:

> I challenge our mission leaders to show their missionaries how to challenge their contacts to read the Book of Mormon and pray about it. Missionaries need to know how to use the Book of Mormon to arouse mankind's interest in studying it, and they need to show how it answers the great questions of the soul. Missionaries need to read with those they teach various passages from the Book of Mormon on gospel subjects.
>
> I challenge our Church writers, teachers, and leaders to tell us more Book of Mormon conversion stories that will strengthen our faith and prepare great missionaries. Show us how to effectively use it as a missionary tool, and let us know how it leads us to Christ and answers our personal problems and those of the world.
>
> I have a vision of home teachers and visiting teachers, ward and branch officers, and stake and mission leaders counseling our people out of the most correct of any book on earth—the Book of Mormon.[5]

Given what President Benson has encouraged us to do, it seems appropriate to use the Book of Mormon as our personal

1. Give us direction in our lives.
2. Gain understanding concerning the ways of the Lord.
3. Help us solve problems.

This concept raises some questions. What type of help is actually available from the scriptures? What are appropriate questions for which we can seek guidance and direction?

I have already quoted Elder Boyd K. Packer as saying:

> In time, I found that the scriptures had answers to things I needed to know . . . that the scriptures are likened to me personally, and that is true of everyone else. . . . I learned that anyone, anywhere, could read in the Book of Mormon and receive inspiration. Some insights came after reading a second, even a third time and seemed to be 'likened' to what I faced in every-day life. . . . When you feel weak, discouraged, depressed, or afraid, open the Book of Mormon and read. Do not let too much time pass before reading a verse, a thought, or a chapter.[6]

We also quoted Elder Henry B. Eyring, who said:

> Sometimes I go to the scriptures for doctrine. Sometimes I go to the scriptures for instruction. I go with a question, and the question usually is "What would God have me do?" or "What would God have me feel?" . . . When we come to a crisis in our life, such as losing a child or spouse, we should go looking in the scriptures for specific help. We will find answers in the scriptures. The Lord seemed to anticipate all of our problems and all of our needs, and He put help in the scriptures for us—if only we seek it."[7]

It seems all of our problems and all of our needs are answered in the scriptures. Whether we are dealing with a major life-changing experience or want to know what to teach in a family home evening lesson, opening our Liahona is an ideal place to start. How vital it is for us to remember to use our Liahona to hear the voice of the Lord! I reiterate again, you'll find the scriptures guide us in three ways:

1. Point the direction we should go.
2. Give us understanding concerning the ways of the Lord.
3. Help us solve the problems we face.

What a remarkable blessing the scriptures become as we apply them personally in our lives.

Notes

1. In Dallin H. Oaks, *The Lord's Way* (Salt Lake City: Deseret Book, 1991), 35.
2. Ibid., 36.
3. Henry B. Eyring, "A Discussion on Scripture Study," *Ensign*, July 2005, 24.
4. Ezra Taft Benson, "Flooding the Earth with the Book of Mormon," *Ensign*, November 1988, 4.
5. Ibid.
6. Boyd K. Packer, "The Book of Mormon: Another Testament of Jesus Christ—Plain and Precious Things," *Ensign*, May 2005, 7–8.
7. Eyring, "A Discussion on Scripture Study," 22–24.

Chapter 6

THE EASY WAY

In the previous chapter, we discussed three ways the Liahona directs us. However, there is another way we need to mention, a way that overrides the entire process of using the Liahona to receive direction in our journey in life. We might think of it as the caution note on the use of a product. That way is the easy way. Alma tells us twice that using the Liahona is easy. "For behold, it is as *easy* to give heed to the word *of* Christ, . . . as it was for our fathers to give heed to this compass" (Alma 37:44; emphasis added).

Then, two verses later he adds, "Do not let us be slothful because of the *easiness* of the way; for so was it with our fathers; for so was it prepared for them, that if they would look they might live; even so it is with us" (Alma 37:46; emphasis added).

Although Alma says the way is easy, he also tells us that Lehi and his family were slothful in that effort and suffered as a result. It appears that if they had given closer heed to their Liahona, Lehi and his family could have avoided some hardship, traveled a more direct course, and not tarried so long in the wilderness. Note what happened to them: "They were slothful and forgot to exercise their faith and diligence and then those marvelous works ceased, and they did not progress in their journey;

"Therefore, they tarried in the wilderness, or did not travel a direct course, and were afflicted with hunger and thirst, because of their transgressions" (Alma 37:41–42).

So, why were they slothful? Why did they forget to exercise faith and diligence?

The word *slothful* is used only four times in the Book of Mormon, three of those describing Lehi's family's use of the Liahona. The fourth use of *slothful* parallels the other three and describes those who would not look at the brass serpent Moses raised up in order to be healed. Why? Because of the "simpleness of the way" (1 Nephi 17:41), a phrase used only once in all of scripture.

So, once again, why was Lehi's family slothful? Why didn't they pay better heed to their Liahona? They had the compass; it seems so easy. Alma gives us the answer: "Because of the easiness of the way" (Alma 37:46), a descriptive phrase that is also used only once in all of scripture. It was simply too easy. The compass was just sitting there, like scriptures on a nightstand.

I had a question somewhere in the back of my mind. When it surfaced, I asked it in my heart. "Does it really work—every time?"

I didn't really doubt that the Liahona Principle was a true principle, because I've had my prayers answered many times in the scriptures. I think my question was more of one asking for a confirmation. And so with those thoughts, I opened my Book of Mormon. It opened right to Alma 37:6-7:

> Now ye may suppose that this is foolishness in me; but behold I say unto you, that by small and simple things are great things brought to pass; and small means in many instances doth confound the wise.
> And the Lord God doth work by means to bring about his great and eternal purposes; and by very small means the Lord doth confound the wise and bringeth about the salvation of many souls.

So what the Lord taught me when I read Alma 37:6-7, what the Spirit impressed upon my heart and mind, was this—it's simple! The tool is simple, and because the Lord God is behind it, it will confound the wise and they won't understand it. It allows God to help us in our times of need and helps accomplish His eternal purposes, to bring about the salvation of our souls. We will bring ourselves to Him as we open our scriptures.

Like looking into the Liahona, opening our scriptures is easy. Sometimes, maybe it's even too easy, and we are slothful and forget to look, or maybe it just seems easier to do something else.

After Lehi was given the Liahona, he and his family followed the directions on the ball. But eventually Nephi's bow broke and his brothers' bows lost their spring, so they could obtain no food. Then came a revelation: "Look upon the ball, and behold the things which are written" (1 Nephi 16:26).

As Lehi looked, he was astonished to learn two new things. First, the pointers worked "according to the faith and diligence and heed which [they] did give unto them" (1 Nephi 16:28), and second, there was "writing, which was plain to be read, which did give [them] understanding concerning the ways of the Lord; and it was written and changed from time to time, according to the faith and diligence which [they] gave unto it" (1 Nephi 16:29).

Maybe it wasn't that looking in the Liahona was too easy. Maybe it was that the direction received was perceived as too hard.

At times, it must have also been easier to do something else, to choose a different direction rather than give heed and diligence to the direction on the Liahona. "For as our fathers were slothful to give heed to this compass . . . they did not prosper" (Alma 37:43).

If the compass said to go over the mountain, maybe it was easier to go around. Whatever it said, Lehi's family did not give heed as they should, because of an apparent alternative way, so they tarried in the wilderness and did not progress in their journey.

So it is with us and our scriptures. It is good to open our scriptures and read. It is even better to personally apply the counsel we are given. Though the way is easy, the application may not be. We may not like the answer.

I always believed that the scriptures were true, and I knew that I needed to live by what was in them. However, I don't think I ever really believed that I could find direct, personal answers for myself and my own individual challenges.

I had been struggling in a major way with overwhelming issues relating to my marriage. I had reached the point of no return; I couldn't do it any longer and had many good reasons that justified my leaving. A friend suggested I look for direction in the scriptures before making such a major decision, and I decided to put it to the test.

I asked Heavenly Father to help me know what I needed to do. Then I opened my scriptures at random. I was a little taken aback by what I started to read. I had turned to Doctrine and Covenants 98 and what I read seemed to be so clearly and directly speaking to me, and me alone. The verses spoke of forgiveness and counseled me to forgive a first, a second, a third, and even a fourth time.

I tried it again and ended up in section 82 of the Doctrine and Covenants, and again I was a bit taken aback because this verse totally supported what I had just read! "Verily, verily, I say unto you, my servants, that inasmuch as you have forgiven one another your trespasses, even so I, the Lord, forgive you" (D&C 82:1).

Two days later I tried it again. I was amazed when I turned to the exact same verses I had turned to the first time. I don't think it was coincidence.

I tend to resist solutions that seem to be too hard or painful, and I was looking for a quick fix. But a quick fix I did not receive. What I did receive is an understanding of what Heavenly Father's will is for me, even though it was not what I thought I wanted and had originally prayed for. I'm not sure exactly how things are going to work out yet, but I am learning that there is help for me individually, and that the scriptures are truly there for me, in a very real sense.

This dear sister had made up her mind to leave her husband. She felt it was the right choice in her journey in life. However, when she opened her Liahona looking for direction, she received a completely different answer. Which way is the easy way—leave her husband or forgive? There are obvious challenges to both.

Exercising faith, diligence, and obedience to the direction we receive from our compass keeps us on the most direct course toward our own promised land. Elder Charles Didier tells us, "To heed and apply what is heard becomes life's perpetual challenge."[1] The true easy way is to seek direction from the Liahona, and then follow the direction given. But it doesn't come without its challenges.

My husband and I were considering becoming foster parents. We felt that the Lord was telling us through feelings of the Holy Ghost that we should. We had already received several feelings that being foster parents would be difficult but that the blessings of doing it would be well worth it to our family. We fasted together one Sunday, asking for guidance from the Lord. At the end of our fast, we prayed as a family and then as a couple.

That evening we were in the living room and I handed the scriptures to my husband, suggesting he ask a question in his mind and open the scriptures. He opened to Doctrine and Covenants 58:4, "For after much tribulation come the blessings."

My husband felt that we should become foster parents; but I struggled more with the decision because the majority of the responsibility would be mine. I felt greatly pestered by the Holy Ghost to do it, yet I also felt a tremendous deal of fear. I was weighed down by the decision and wanted more guidance. I prayed about it more. I then sat down on the couch and opened the scriptures, and my eyes went right to Doctrine and Covenants 78:13: "Behold, this is the preparation wherewith I prepare you, and the foundation, and the ensample which I give unto you, whereby you may accomplish the commandments which are given you."

I felt peaceful, and as I thought about it, I became hopeful that this scripture meant I could relax for a while and "prepare" to do foster care someday. The next day the Lord set me straight.

I was sitting in the car and took the Book of Mormon out of the glove box to see if the Lord had more to say to me. I opened to 2 Nephi 32:7:

"And now I, Nephi, cannot say more; the Spirit stoppeth mine utterance, and I am left to mourn because of the unbelief, and the wickedness, and the ignorance, and the stiffneckedness of men; for they will not search knowledge, nor understand great knowledge, when it is given unto them in plainness, even as plain as word can be."

I wondered if perhaps this wasn't really an answer for me. I flipped the book open again, this time to a scripture about sharing the gospel. I thought that was interesting because, by law, you cannot push your religion onto foster children, but they do learn simply by being around your family. This had been one of my fears.

I opened the Book of Mormon one more time. It opened straight to 2 Nephi 32:7 again. "Okay," I thought, "I get the message."

However, the fear I felt about what becoming foster parents might do to my family was overwhelming. One minute I felt fine about it, but the next minute I began thinking about all of the horrible things that could happen. My mind would reel with this fear that almost took my breath away. I knew the Lord was asking us to be foster parents, but in order to do that, I needed to put aside

the powerful fear I felt and place absolute trust in Him. This was the hardest decision I had ever faced.

I decided to trust the Lord and just do it. Yet the same night I made this decision, I still felt anxiety. I said a prayer in my heart: "We have decided to become foster parents. Could I please have peace from the Holy Ghost now?" A thought came into my head: "You don't have your foster parent papers in yet." I finished my papers that night, and my family members finished theirs by the next day.

Two days later I realized that the pestering from the Holy Ghost had ended, and surprisingly, so had the intense fear. I still felt normal concern, but the overwhelming fears I had felt earlier were gone. I believe the Lord gave us many strong answers during this time to help us reach the right decision, because He knew Satan was fighting to stop us. We are now foster parents and have enjoyed doing this challenging but rewarding work for the Lord's children.

Exercising faith, diligence, and obedience to the direction we receive from our scriptural Liahona is truly the easy way, the one true way that allows us to prosper and progress in our journey, and carries us into a far better land of promise.

Notes
  1. Charles Didier, "Man's Search for Divine Truth," *Ensign*, November 2005, 48.

Chapter 7

HOW TO USE
YOUR LIAHONA

In the introduction, I encouraged you to think of where you are at in life, identify your major challenges or struggles, and then open your Book of Mormon with those in mind. I then suggested you read a verse or two on the page you turned to and apply what you read personally to your situation.

If you have not yet done that, now would be an ideal time to stop reading and open your Liahona. There is no right or wrong place. Simply open your Book of Mormon and apply what you read to where you are at in life or to a question you have. If you gain insight at this point, that's great; if you don't, that's okay too.

Again, we find many sources of inspiration and direction. The scriptures are only one but they are one of the most powerful. As you use your Liahona, insights or inspiration will come; you might possibly receive confirmation of revelation you've already received from other sources. If appropriate, what you receive will be in accordance with the law of witnesses, which states, "In the mouth of two or three witnesses shall every word be established" (2 Corinthians 13:1, D&C 6:28).

This law means that, on important issues, you will receive needed inspiration two or three times, so you are certain it comes from Heavenly Father. Elder Gene R. Cook tells the conversion story of a Protestant minister friend of his, which demonstrates how this law works:

> Brother Smith said that after confirmation of the truth [of the Book of Mormon] had come to him by the Spirit, he had received added assurance through a familiar means—inspiration to turn to specific scriptural references.
>
> This had happened to him before. In times past when he had been studying the Bible or preaching, he had found that a particular biblical reference—such as Isaiah 6:7—might suddenly come into his mind. When he looked up the scripture, he would find that it dealt with the very topic or problem at hand. Because this had worked for him so frequently, he determined to try the same test with latter-day scriptures.
>
> He prayed, "Father, if this book is true—and I'm feeling these feelings confirming that it is—then help me know that it is, talking with me through the scriptures the way thou hast done in the Bible." Immediately flashed into his mind D&C 17:3. He looked up the scripture: "And after that you have obtained faith, and have seen them [the Book of Mormon plates or, in his instance, the printed Book of Mormon] with your eyes, you shall testify of them, by the power of God."
>
> Deeply moved by that response, he nevertheless asked, "Lord, wouldst thou do it one more time,

as thou hast said that in the mouth of two or three witnesses shall every word be established." Immediately Alma 13:6 came to his mind: "And thus being called by this holy calling, and ordained unto the high priesthood of the holy order of God, to teach his commandments unto the children of men, that they also might enter into his rest. . . ." He then felt a strong witness that the Lord was calling him to a holy calling in the true Church and that he would be ordained to the high priesthood in order to teach the Lord's commandments to the children of men.

Then he prayed again humbly, as did Gideon, "Let not thine anger be hot against me" (Judges 6:39), and asked the Lord to give him just one more witness that he was truly deciding correctly. As he prayed, a reference came into his mind—Moroni 6:3: "And none were received unto baptism save they took upon them the name of Christ, having a determination to serve him to the end." That verse, and the verses immediately surrounding it, pressed heavily upon him and convinced him that he must be baptized and be "cleansed by the power of the Holy Ghost" (Moroni 6:4).[1]

This brother received the needed witnesses to know of a surety what God would have him do. In his case, these witnesses came through the prompting of specific verses for him to turn to. But for each of us, those witnesses can come in many different ways. Our scriptural Liahona should be one of the first places we look. These sacred words have carefully been preserved to show us the course we should travel, just as the Liahona "was prepared to show unto our fathers the course which they should travel in the wilderness . . . for so was it prepared for them, that if they would look they might live" (Alma 37:39, 46)

✳

I awoke around four o'clock in the morning and realized it would be my fifth day of constant pain. My shoulders had huge knots in them, the cords on either side of my neck were screaming, it hurt to touch my hair, my back felt like I had a new sunburn, and the right side of my body from the hip to the toes was tingling and achy and numb. I had used loads of muscle relaxants, painkillers, medicated salve, and ice packs. I was tired of lying in bed and hurting every time I tried to move.

As I lay there sick and tired of it all, I was ready to try anything. The only thing I could think of that I hadn't done was to read the scriptures. It's amazing, isn't it? The scriptures had helped me countless times before, but the last thing I thought of in this intense pain was to read the scriptures.

I lay there contemplating those very thoughts and knew I had to ask forgiveness for my laziness and for relying on the Lord only as my last resort. How silly. How sad! I said a prayer, knowing I was unworthy to even ask for help, yet also knowing that if I didn't ask, He couldn't bless me.

After the prayer, I simply opened my scriptures, and they fell open to Doctrine and Covenants 108.

I had been there before; I had previously underlined some of the words in red. To my amazement, the words flowed off the page:

> Your sins are forgiven you, because you have obeyed my voice in coming up hither this morning . . . . Let your soul be at rest concerning your spiritual standing, and resist no more my voice. Arise up and be more careful in observing your vows, which you have made . . . and you shall be blessed with exceeding great blessings. Wait patiently . . . then you shall be remembered . . . if you continue faithful. . . . And behold, and lo, I am with you to bless you and deliver you forever Amen. (D&C 108:1–8)

A flood of peace washed over me as I lay there, awed at my answer from a loving and patient Father. I was reminded once again that He knew me and my situation, and He was ready to bless me if only I would ask. I wiped away my tears with a sweet smile and prepared to meet the day knowing my pain would go away and I could face anything—because my Father still loved me.

✷

This dear sister has learned to greatly appreciate the scriptures, and she turns to them often for help. How does she do it? How does she apply the Liahona Principle to receive the direction she needs? The process is easy and entails three simple steps:

1. Have something in mind.
2. Open your scriptures.
3. Apply what you read.

Let's look at these three steps a little closer.

1. HAVE SOMETHING IN MIND

Are you looking for direction, understanding, enlightenment, or help with a problem? If so, think of that thing. The more specific you are, the more specific your answer can be. Like Elder Eyring, you might also think, "What would God have me do?" or "What would God have me feel?"

2. OPEN YOUR SCRIPTURES, AND READ A VERSE OR TWO

You can read during your daily reading schedule, randomly open the book, or simply let the book fall open. Much of the time, your answer will be in the first verse or two that you read, though you may read more to get a bigger picture. Remember, we should turn to the Book of Mormon most often, but other scriptures, including general conference talks, also offer opportunities for revelation.

3. APPLY WHAT YOU READ TO YOUR QUESTION OR THOUGHT IN MIND

It is in the personal application of the scriptures that enlightenment comes. Who are you in the scriptures you are reading? How do the words describe you or your situation? What do you learn about you or your situation? Where are you at? What do you need to do?

As you apply these three simple steps, you will find the promised direction, understanding, and help that your Liahona has to offer. That answer will often give you the insight described in chapter 2, answers to the questions "Where am I at?" and "What should I do?" Frequently, you may need to open the scriptures more than once in order to get the full answer. If the answer is not easily discernable, be patient and open your Liahona the next day, looking for more understanding. As the elder in chapter 2 wrote, "The key is to find out how the scriptures apply in my life, rather than if they apply." It may take a little practice to learn to use your scriptures this way, but most of the time, the answers are surprisingly clear.

I had a wonderful experience on my mission with opening up the Book of Mormon. I had been taught that if I wanted answers from the Lord, I needed to open up my scriptures and recognize the verses I read as my answer. We had an investigator who was struggling to accept some of the commitments of the gospel, so we decided to suggest this to her at our next discussion.

Linda was the most golden investigator a missionary could hope for. We met Linda through Church members Mark and Roxanne. Roxanne set up times for us to come over and teach Linda at their house. Linda progressed wonderfully in the gospel—she loved to read the scriptures, she enjoyed going to church and Relief Society activities, and she had committed to be baptized with her daughters. Unfortunately, we found that she was living with a man she loved, but because of a previous bad marriage, she had not found the courage to marry him.

As missionaries, we were unsure what to tell Linda, other than to share our testimonies and teach her the doctrine. Mark and Roxanne were both converts and were able to share their conversion stories, but neither had gone through Linda's experience. As a result, Linda was left to struggle through this difficult decision. She had been praying but hadn't received an answer definitive and strong enough for her to act upon. Because we didn't know what else to do—and maybe it should have been the first thing we did—we decided to teach Linda about opening up the scriptures to find an answer.

Linda was nervous about doing this and asked each of us to open our scriptures too. She said a prayer and opened her Book of Mormon. As her eyes fell on the page, she gave a little scream and slammed the book shut! That was a response I had never experienced, and I was unsure what to do! Thankfully, the Spirit prompted me to ask if I could guess what she opened to. She consented, and again with the Spirit's prompting, I asked if she had opened to Alma 39.

She had. The first words her eyes had landed on were in the chapter heading: "Sexual sin is an abomination." Linda knew that she needed a very blunt answer in order to choose the path that was the hardest to follow, and the Lord obliged. He also knew that was what she needed.

Linda had received her answer, and she knew without any doubt what the Lord wanted her to do. It was a wonderful, testimony-building experience for all those involved. If we want to speak with the Lord and ask questions, we go to Him in prayer. If we want to hear His voice, we can go to the scriptures. In the scriptures, He has already revealed His will to us. We must simply open the scriptures to find answers to our prayers.

As testified to by this missionary, our answers are in the scriptures. It is our privilege to open the scriptures and learn where we are and what Heavenly Father would have us know or do.

Someone unfamiliar with finding answers in the scriptures in this manner may be uncertain or hesitant to try this process. The elder who shared his experience above makes an excellent observation: "If I wanted answers from the Lord, I needed to open up my scriptures and recognize the verses I read as my answer."

The way is that simple, that easy. When we open up the scriptures with a question in mind, the verses we read are our answer. We don't keep opening the scriptures looking for a different answer or a better answer. As we become comfortable with the process, and more familiar with the scriptures, we gain more and more insights.

I had always heard people talk about opening the scriptures and finding verses that answered their prayers. I even heard stories about scriptures falling open to the right place and lives being blessed and changed. I didn't doubt this happened, but I figured it was reserved for a special few who had huge problems with important decisions to make.

There came a time in my life when I was struggling with where I needed to be and what I needed to be doing. I was at BYU—Idaho and I enjoyed many things there, but I felt that it wasn't right to stay. I had no idea what to do. Changing colleges—especially in the middle of the school year—would be difficult, but I felt I shouldn't be there any longer.

A good friend suggested that I visit a different school to explore my options. She even suggested a university, but I had always sworn I would never go to that school! At this point, though, I actually considered it. I did my homework on the programs, costs, and so on. Though I knew I could transfer, I wasn't sure if that was the right thing to do. It would take a lot of courage for me to leave behind all of my friends and everything I knew to go to a new place. I also knew there would be opposition and disapproval in going to this university. This was not a decision I took lightly.

My friend counseled me to find out what God wanted me to do and then just do it and have faith. I determined to do just that. I went into my room, closed the door, and knelt down. I told God that I wanted to know what He wanted me to do, and I would do it, no matter how difficult it might be.

I stayed there until an answer came, but it was not the answer I had expected: Look in the scriptures. This didn't exactly answer my question but I knew that was what I needed to do to find my answer.

I got up and sat on the bed with my scriptures in hand. I said a prayer in my heart for guidance as I remembered all of the stories I had always heard. I decided to give it a shot. I opened my scriptures, and the book fell open to a page; my eyes were drawn to one specific verse. I read it, and it touched my soul. I said a prayer of gratitude and decided to try again.

Once more the scriptures opened to a specific verse that spoke to me. I continued to read and flip open my scriptures, and each time, the verses spoke to me. I knew that God had answered my prayer many times over. He gave me the answers I needed, and they gave me the courage to make a big change in my life. Times were not always easy after that, but this experience helped me to see that my decision was right. Only then did I have the courage to continue on, knowing what God wanted me to do.

I learned from this experience that God can and does speak to us through the scriptures but we have to open them and truly believe that we can find His answers. As we open them often in prayer, we will know God's will for us.

In summary, we can follow three simple steps to use our scriptural Liahona to reveal information. Those steps are:

1. Have something in mind.
2. Open the scriptures.
3. Apply what is read.

Our scriptural Liahona reveals three types of information, which are:

1. The direction in which to go.
2. Understanding the ways of the Lord.
3. Help in solving problems.

As you follow these steps, you may want to write down your experiences in a journal or notebook. By writing them down, you will understand better what you have received, and you will solidify your answer. These personal revelations and instructions may be as important to you as Lehi's were to him.

Notes

1. Gene R. Cook, "Moroni's Promise," *Ensign*, April 1994, 12.

Chapter 8
FOURFOLD RESPONSIBILITY

President Gordon B. Hinckley gave the following counsel, saying that "each of us has a fourfold responsibility. First, we have a responsibility to our families. Second, we have a responsibility to our employers. Third, we have a responsibility to the Lord's work. Fourth, we have a responsibility to ourselves."[1]

The stories I have shared in the previous six chapters are all about people looking for answers in those four areas: family, employment, Church, and self. Those four roles cover most of our concerns in life and therefore most of the reasons we would turn to our Liahona. The next four chapters contain more stories of people who have turned to the scriptures to find answers to the questions they have had. There is one chapter for various aspects of each of these four responsibilities.

Personal experience profoundly teaches and touches the soul, for it is something we can all relate to. My desire is that as you read these stories, they will inspire your soul, encourage you to make better use of the Liahona you have been given, and help you understand better what God's plan is for you.

A few years ago, our stake presidency suggested that we open the Book of Mormon to find answers to our prayers. This rang true to me—I had already had this experience once while on my mission. Over the next few years, many members of the stake had good experiences doing this, and my mind was opened up to the possibility of using this technique more often. I started on a journey that has since changed my life.

I have found that each time there is something I need the Lord's help with—something that I have prayed and fasted about—the answer can come in a powerful way by opening the scriptures.

This is how it has worked for me: I pray and ask the Lord my question and then I take the scriptures and open them up. I let my eyes go to a verse and read it. Sometimes one verse is my answer; sometimes it is several verses or a whole chapter. Sometimes a few verses prior to the first verse I look at also apply, but the verse my eyes go to is always my main answer. As I read it, I recognize that the words fit directly with what I have asked about, and I recognize it as an answer.

Often I receive a strong answer and can feel the clarity of the words enter my heart as I read. I know it's an answer from the Lord to me. Occasionally, I open to a verse that I need to think about for a few days, yet it rings true and stays in my mind and I know I have received an answer from the Lord. Sometimes if I just open the book to see if the Lord has anything to say to me, I won't open to anything important—but if it's something I've prayed about and prepared for, the answer always comes.

I have received a lot of answers through the Book of Mormon. I have also received answers from the other books of scripture. Anything that is the word of the Lord through His inspired servants can come directly into your heart as His answer.

Notes

1. Gordon B. Hinckley, "Rejoicing in the Privilege to Serve," June 2003 Worldwide Leadership Broadcast, 22.

Chapter 9
RESPONSIBILITY TO FAMILY AND FRIENDS

President Gordon B. Hinckley tells us the first responsibility we have is to our families. In a worldwide leadership broadcast, he said, "It is imperative that you not neglect your families. Nothing you have is more precious.... When all is said and done, it is this family relationship which we will take with us into the life beyond."[1]

The scriptures are one of the most important tools Heavenly Father has given us to lead our families into that "life beyond." Alma provides counsel, even a promise, that is so applicable to families.

> For behold, it is as easy to give heed to the word of Christ, which will point to you a straight course to eternal bliss, as it was for our fathers to give heed to this compass, which would point unto them a straight course to the promised land.
>
> And now I say, is there not a type in this thing? For just as surely as this director did bring our fathers, by following its course, to the promised land, shall the words of Christ, if we follow their course, carry us beyond this vale of sorrow into a far better land of promise. (Alma 37:44–45)

As we open our Liahona, direction, understanding, and help will come to show us how to lead our families back to our Father in Heaven. Along with our families, there is a natural and compelling desire to include our friends as well.

The following stories show a few ways the scriptures have helped in family and friend relationships.

THEY WILL BELIEVE

At one time we were experiencing some pretty drastic challenges with one of our children. We had prayed and fasted and gone to the temple seeking answers about how to help her. One day when I was in the temple chapel, I opened the scriptures to see if I could receive direction. I opened to Doctrine and Covenants 31:2. It read, "Behold, you have had many afflictions because of your family; nevertheless, I will bless you and your family, yea, your little ones; and the day cometh that they will believe and know the truth and be one with you in my church."

Of course this scripture brought tears to my eyes—and my husband's, when I shared it with him. It didn't give us an answer about what specifically to do for our daughter, but it did let us know that Heavenly Father was aware of the situation and that He had heard our prayers. He knew that our hearts were sad and broken, and He promised us that He would bless us and our children! It didn't say how or when but just that the day would come, in His time, that all would be well. This scripture helped me to take a lot of the responsibility for "fixing" the situation off my own shoulders and let the Lord carry it, like He said He would.

THEY ANSWERED NOTHING

Though I love my family, most of them are not members of the Church, and many of them have very negative feelings toward the Church. Many times I have wanted to say something, to bear my testimony and share my feelings. But each time I have tried, it has not been a positive experience.

One time we had an impromptu get-together with extended family members. It seemed like an ideal time to speak up, to say something about the Church, to let them know of restored gospel truths, but I couldn't bring myself to do it. It bothered me that I couldn't share my feelings or my testimony with them.

I took my concerns to Heavenly Father, explaining to Him how I really wanted to help my family. I then took the "opening the Book of Mormon" challenge, looking for direction or help about how to do this.

The Book of Mormon opened to the story of Alma and Amulek watching their converts and records being burned, and the whole time keeping their mouths shut as they were imprisoned, beaten, starved, and persecuted for doing no wrong. When the judge asked, "What say ye for yourselves? . . . It came to pass that Alma and Amulek answered him nothing." Three days later, in prison and in response to the questioning of many lawyers, judges, priests, and teachers, "They answered them nothing." Then the chief judge appeared before them again, commanding them to speak, "But they answered nothing" (Alma 14:17–19).

I learned from these verses that the time to say something had not yet arrived. There are times I need to keep my mouth shut and trust in our Heavenly Father to take care of everything else.

ABRAHAM'S TEST

When my son James was about a year and a half old, he became extremely sick. He had a high fever and was very weak. I tried everything I knew of to help him recover. Several different doctors had seen him, and his father had given him a blessing, but he wasn't getting any better. I desperately watched as my baby got weaker and weaker. I could feel his will to survive also getting weaker and weaker.

His father gave him another blessing, but he still made no improvement. I felt him slipping away, and there was nothing I could do to stop it. I had taken him to the emergency room, and there was nothing that they could do. The medicine they prescribed did nothing. I felt like I was losing my baby. I was desperate. I turned to my scriptures, opening to Genesis 22:2: "And he said, Take now thy son, thine only son Isaac, whom thou lovest, and get thee into the land of Moriah; and offer him there for a burnt offering upon one of the mountains which I will tell thee of."

My heart sank. I didn't want to be an Abraham. I didn't want to be given that test. After reading more of the chapter, I knew what I had to do. I didn't have to sacrifice my son, but I had to be willing to give him back to our Father. I wasn't able to accept that concept. I tried to ignore what the scripture had said, trying again to help him with medicine. That night I couldn't sleep; I felt a great uneasiness. I was afraid that if I was willing to sacrifice my son, God would take him from me. I felt an overwhelming desperation to hang onto my son.

Finally, after much struggling, I resigned myself to trust in the Lord's will and agreed to sacrifice my son to him. As soon as I did, a feeling of peace came over me and the struggle was over. Immediately after, James's fever broke and he began to regain his strength.

Since that time, I have been reminded continually by the Spirit of the sacrifice that I agreed to make, that I would place my trust in the will of God.

BE OF GOOD CHEER

I share a poignant moment in my life when I sought the Lord in prayer with all my heart. I was passing through my own personal Gethsemane. In body and spirit I was sick and wounded, and I truly felt that I would not survive the pain.

On a Monday afternoon, I had come home and found that my young son had taken his own life. He was fifteen years old. He was loved so very deeply, and I yearned for the miracle of life to be restored to him. I wanted his presence in my home; I wanted his kisses, his hugs, his laughter, his mission, his temple marriage, and his children to be part of my future. With his death, I experienced a death of all my dreams for him and the death of my personal dreams for the future because of the vital role he played in our lives.

When my beloved son died, my world changed in one day. Gone forever was the life I knew and loved. I had to learn to live in a new world.

In my personal "Sacred Grove," I at first struggled with the question "Why did this happen?" I spent sleepless nights that stretched to weeks and months, wondering how I could survive feeling so lonely, afraid, sick, oppressed, and brokenhearted. Then I asked a relentless round of what-ifs. These questions were never answered.

From the Spirit, I learned I was asking the wrong questions. I needed to ask another question. Instead of "why?" or "what if?" I needed to ask, "What can I learn from this experience?"

The answer to this question has determined the quality of my life since and helps me face tomorrow—and the eternities to come. The Lord expects us to move forward in faith no matter what the difficulty or sorrow.

I recall reading the charge in the scriptures to be of good cheer: "And now, verily I say unto you, and what I say unto one I say unto all, be of good cheer, little children; for I am in your midst, and I have not forsaken you" (D&C 61:36). I remember the Spirit whispering to me that that meant me too.

I found I had much to be joyful for. I found that my love for my son continued to grow day by day; I rejoiced in being his mother. It was a rich and satisfying moment when the first year passed and we went to the temple, where my husband did our son's temple work.

I have felt the veil become thin and have felt the presence of my son often. I feel his love for our family, and we know that he is engaged in learning and working in the spirit world.

Like Joseph sharing his experiences of time spent in his Sacred Grove, I can bear testimony from personal experience that the Lord does indeed answer prayers; we can believe His word and we can trust His grace.

CONTENTION IS NOT OF ME

I grew up in a family and extended family that fought about many things. Even as a child, I couldn't understand how adults didn't know certain topics of conversation would cause loud contention. I knew that the discussion of politics or religion caused turmoil and upset people. Over time, I grew to dislike the times we spent visiting certain family members.

As I grew up and married, I simply avoided spending time with those family members altogether. But some of these people were my closest family, and I could not always avoid contact. Some of that contention was aimed at me for choosing a different direction than others in my family. I have a loving relationship with my husband and children, and at times, it has caused envy and contempt.

One evening during a family gathering, I was deeply concerned about something that was said. I was on the verge of responding in a way that would make the situation worse. I came home from the visit in turmoil because I was so upset and angry. I wanted to defend myself against the constant criticism I felt. As I went to bed, I prayed for guidance. I could not get to sleep, so in the late hours of the night, I finally got out of bed and picked up my scriptures.

I loved my family and wanted to be able to help them understand my feelings—without the contention that always seemed to be there when a difference of ideas was expressed. I asked Heavenly Father to help me find a way to do this. I began flipping through my Book of Mormon and found my answer in 3 Nephi 11:29: "For verily, verily I say unto you, he that hath the spirit of contention is not of me, but is of the devil, who is the father of contention, and he stirreth up the hearts of men to contend with anger, one with another."

I learned that by responding in anger or hurt, I would only fuel contention. So now, I simply don't let my feathers get ruffled—on the outside, anyway—and I try to keep my cool. The contention has not yet gone away, and we still have differences of opinion expressed with criticism and anger, but now I can say that I feel better for not participating. I understand myself better because I took the time to try to understand why I felt angry or upset, and I no longer respond negatively.

HUMBLE THYSELF

Last Sunday in Church I was pondering a situation with a family member whom I love very much that seemed insurmountable. To me, it was a critical problem that had me feeling cornered with no way out. The statement "I was beside myself" fit my state of mind well.

During the sacrament, I picked up my Book of Mormon, held it tightly, and said a prayer. I told my Father in Heaven I needed help and that I knew my answer was somewhere in that wonderful book. Then I let the book fall open. It opened to Alma 32:41: "But if ye will nourish the word, yea, nourish the tree as it beginneth to grow, by your faith with great diligence, and with patience, looking forward to the fruit thereof, it shall take root; and behold it shall be a tree springing up unto everlasting life."

This verse immediately calmed my soul. I knew I needed to have patience and faith and continue to nourish the tree as best I could.

This scripture told me what I needed to strive to do. Now I needed to know how to do that. Past lessons had taught me that, to find the real problem, we need to open the scriptures. Then, in order to find the solution, we often need to open the scriptures again!

With that in mind, I opened my Book of Mormon and read. The first three verses of the chapter on the page spoke of persecutions of the righteous and how King Mosiah sent a proclamation throughout the land forbidding further persecutions. The sacrament ended, and I closed the book, thinking I would ponder it more after church. Suddenly, a thought came very strongly into my mind: I needed to read more than three verses! I needed to know what those who felt persecuted did to overcome their trials! Unfortunately, I hadn't noticed what chapter it was, or even what book it was in.

I again said a prayer that I would be able to find that page again. I thought about looking up "persecution" in the Topical Guide. But first I glanced down at my Book of Mormon, letting it fall open again. It fell open to the exact same page—Mosiah 27. Later, as I read further in the chapter, I realized the message had to do with being humble. This was my answer, and it has helped me. I need to humble myself before the Lord and have patience and faith and know that things will work out.

LET THY LOVE BE FOR THEM AS THYSELF

I have always been blessed to have many good LDS friends. The group of friends I hung out with in my senior year consisted of several of us who had met and become friends the previous year. By the time the middle of senior year rolled around, some of us were starting to get on each others' nerves, particularly David.

David constantly made negative, degrading comments toward us. His pessimism and cutting comments were so unlike him, but once he started, he didn't stop. As the days passed and the unkind remarks continued, we became offended and bitter, especially because he didn't even seem to care that he was hurting us.

After weeks of praying, which resulted in no change, a few of us decided to fast one day and go to the temple to do baptisms so we would know how to handle the situation. While in the temple [are these high school seniors; did they go to baptisms for the dead or what?], we opened to the following, which spoke unmistakably to us.

> Be thou humble; and the Lord thy God shall lead thee by the hand, and give thee answers to thy prayers. *I know thy heart, and have heard thy prayers concerning thy brethren. Be not partial towards them in love above many others, but let thy love be for them* as for thyself; and let thy love abound unto all men, and unto all who love my name. (D&C 112:10–11; emphasis added)

We realized that it was not our job to change David. We were only supposed to love him as Christ would, and pray for him. We needed to stop focusing on the bad and look to the good person David really was. We were letting his faults and weaknesses overshadow his strengths. We needed to forgive him as we wanted others to forgive us. We needed to be submissive, meek, humble, patient, long-suffering, and to pray to Heavenly Father for help. All along the real problem was with us—not David. We felt bad that we had been so foolish and prideful, and we were grateful for the reminder from the scriptures to always strive for that Christlike love.

On the way home from the temple we discussed what we had felt and agreed to put forth a new effort to be kind, patient, and positive with David, and to continue to be prayerful. We also decided that whenever we noticed anything good about him, we would share it with the others to help build him up in our eyes again. Then we each took a turn and said a prayer of thanks, asking for continued help and guidance in the following weeks.

SWALLOWED UP IN THE GREAT DEEP

When my oldest daughter turned fifteen, we realized she was heavily into drug and alcohol use. It was to the point that she was flunking school and not participating in any productive way as part of our family. At the time I was the Young Women president, and I was feeling hopeless. It seemed every time I taught a lesson, I ended up in tears. My daughter was placed in a treatment center twice and "flunked out" both times. Soon she was sent to a state facility for wayward girls and she spent her junior year of high school there. We learned during the course of this stay that she had turned away from nearly every value we had tried to teach her.

I felt like a complete failure as a mother, and didn't care much about being a wife to my husband or a mother to our two other daughters. I was frantic in my search for answers.

I had to teach a lesson in Young Women one Sunday and had no idea what I was going to teach. I decided to try the Liahona Principle to see if it would give me an idea. I opened my Book of Mormon, and it fell open to Ether 2:25, which read, "And behold, I prepare you against these things; for ye cannot cross this great deep save I prepare you against the waves of the sea, and the winds which have gone forth, and the floods which shall come. Therefore what will ye that I should prepare for you that ye may have light when ye are swallowed up in the depths of the sea?"

I taught that lesson to my young women—about preparing themselves against the "great deep." I can honestly say, as Joseph Smith said, "Never did any passage of scripture come with more power to the heart of man than this did at this time to mine" (Joseph Smith—History 1:12).

I have never been a scriptorian; I never felt I could teach from the scriptures alone. I needed a manual for every lesson I taught. But as I taught from that one verse alone, I was able to develop a forty-five-minute lesson. Most of all, it sank deep into my heart, and I realized that I only needed to ask the Lord for help so I would not be "swallowed up" in my self-pity, fear, and sense of sorrow.

This was truly the beginning of my dedication to scripture study. Before that time, I had not realized the help that was there for me. It never seemed so personal to me.

Two years later, when my second daughter quit seminary during her senior year, I knew she too was leaving the arms of the gospel and choosing a different path. I turned to the scriptures, looking for something—anything—and my Book of Mormon fell open to 3 Nephi 18:20, which read, "And whatsoever ye shall ask the Father in my name, which is right, believing that ye shall receive, behold it shall be given unto you."

It has been nearly three years since that day in January of 2003 but I have remembered that scripture. It speaks to me of faith and diligence in continuing to ask for those blessings that are righteous. I have tried so hard to let my faith replace my fears for my sweet daughters. They are not yet active in the Church, and I have come to terms with the fact that they may never be in the course of this lifetime. But I have been able to have the faith that all will be well. They are wonderful, honest, compassionate, and bright girls.

I have a third daughter who seems to be "at home" in the gospel. I believe it is because her mother has learned, through these lessons, the importance of the scriptures as a guide in our lives. I know that the Book of Mormon is written for our day, to help us solve our problems, and I am grateful to have learned this principle of looking to the scriptures for answers.

Notes
1. Gordon B. Hinckley, "Rejoicing in the Privilege to Serve," June 2003 Worldwide Leadership Broadcast, 22.

Chapter 10
RESPONSIBILITY TO EMPLOYER/EDUCATION

President Gordon B. Hinckley tells us the second responsibility we have is to our business or employer. I would add education, if that is the stage of life we are in. In counsel he gave to bishops, which is applicable to all of us, he said, "You must not rob your employer of the time and energy that are rightfully his. You must not rob your family of time which belongs to them. . . . It is possible to budget your time so that you neglect neither your employer, your family, nor your flock."[1]

As we juggle our responsibilities, we will find direction, under-standing, and help from our scriptural Liahona.

BEHOLD, HE WAS A MAN

I was at our stake's youth conference. A half hour had been set aside for everyone to find an isolated spot to study scriptures, meditate, and reflect on the things that had been taught. When I went out on my own, I was determined to get something out of it.

As I sat down with my Book of Mormon in hand, my mind started thinking of all the workshops I had attended that day, all of which had dealt somehow with the last days. As I was pondering, I realized that, because I was starting college in the fall, this was my last youth conference and, in a way, my last days. I thought about how I was leaving where I had spent my whole life, and I began to think of all the changes in store. Even though I had been excited at the prospect of moving on and beginning the rest of my life, the closeness of it all now seemed kind of scary to me.

So, while thinking about how I had no idea where my life was going to lead me in a few months, and pondering all the warnings and signs of the last days, I opened my Book of Mormon with a prayer in my heart that I would receive something—anything—to comfort me or give me advice on what to do.

My Book of Mormon fell open to Alma 48:15, a verse that told me that because of the Nephites' strong faith and obedience to the commandments, God had allowed them to prosper and be pro-tected in the land. Verses 15 and 16 explained that God didn't just protect the Nephites, he specifically told them what to do, where to go, where to send their armies, and where to set up defenses.

I knew then that if I strived to have faith and keep the com-mandments, God wouldn't desert me but would protect me. Not only would He protect me, He would also guide me, so I would always know what to do and never have reason to fear.

Verse 17 then states, "If all men had been, and were, and ever would be, like unto Moroni, behold, the very powers of hell would have been shaken forever; yea, the devil would never have power over the hearts of the children of men."

This helped me with what I had already read. It told me to follow Moroni's example and there would be no reason to fear because the devil could never have power over me. My mind wanted to make an excuse and reason that I couldn't be like Moroni because he was too great, but verse 18 wouldn't allow me to make that excuse: "Behold, he was a man."

Because the scriptures observed that Moroni was nothing more than a man, I knew that I was capable of following his example. I couldn't have asked for better words of comfort to help me know what to do to prepare for everything I'd face in the near future.

ARM OF FLESH

Never before have my prayers been answered so literally.

I was in the shower enjoying its soothing warmth. My forearm was sore from my elbow to my wrist with tendonitis caused by a combination of too much work and a lot of golf. I stood there under the spray, pondering. Many things raced through my mind. "The bills are stacking up, and there's not enough money to pay them all. Ow, my elbow hurts! The house is a mess. Will we ever get the second bathroom put back together? Things at work are piling up—looks like more long hours today. And my sore arm . . . it aches so much, and I still have to get through the whole rest of the day."

I thought about how much better I could be doing at so many things. And though I tried and I tried, I couldn't seem to catch up. I had been praying for weeks for help from the Lord. Then between rinsing and repeating, my thoughts changed.

I had been reading the Book of Mormon every day, as a challenge from my friends, trying to finish it by year's end. However, I had fallen behind schedule. So a few days earlier, I had picked up the book to try and catch up. I opened the scriptures to read 2 Nephi 4; the scriptures filled my mind and the Spirit touched me when I read these passages:

O wretched man that I am! Yea, my heart sorroweth because of my flesh; my soul grieveth because of mine iniquities. I am encompassed about, because of the temptations and the sins which do so easily beset me. And when I desire to rejoice, my heart groaneth because of my sins; nevertheless, I know in whom I have trusted.

My God hath been my support; he hath led me through mine afflictions in the wilderness; and he hath preserved me upon the waters of the great deep. He hath filled me with his love, even unto the consuming of my flesh. He hath confounded mine enemies, unto the causing of them to quake before me.

Behold, he hath heard my cry by day. . . . I waxed bold in mighty prayer before him; yea, my voice have I sent up on high. . . . And [His Spirit] has ministered unto me. And mine eyes have beheld great things . . . if the Lord in his condescension unto the children of men hath visited [me] in so much mercy, why should my heart weep and my soul linger in the valley of sorrow, and my flesh waste away, and my strength slacken, because of mine afflictions? (2 Nephi 4:17–26)

Why indeed? I thought. Then as I remembered the rest of Nephi's words, it hit me. Two days earlier, the Spirit had spoken and it took me until now to listen. Nephi continues:

Awake, my soul! No longer droop in sin. Rejoice, O my heart, and give place no more for the enemy of my soul. Do not anger again because of mine enemies. Do not slacken my strength because of mine afflictions. . . . O Lord, wilt thou redeem my soul? Wilt thou deliver me out of the hands of mine enemies? Wilt thou make me that I may shake at the appearance of sin? . . . O Lord, I have trusted in thee, and I will trust in thee forever. I will not put my trust in the *arm* of flesh; for I know that cursed is he that putteth his trust in the *arm* of flesh. Yea, cursed is he that putteth his trust in man or maketh flesh his *arm*. (2 Nephi 4:28–29, 31, 34; emphasis added)

Now each ache of my arm, each pain of my flesh, became a prick in my heart as I realized where I had put my trust. As I struggled through that day with more aches and pains, I was humbled. Prompted to get a priesthood blessing, I called on a good friend and member of our bishopric. In this blessing, the Lord promised that I would be able to provide for my family both physically and spiritually. There were no admonitions, no I-told-you-so's, only a calm, peaceful feeling that the Lord loves me. I felt as Nephi did when he wrote, "Rejoice, O my heart, and cry unto the Lord, and say: O Lord, I will praise thee forever; yea, my soul will rejoice in thee, my God, and the rock of my salvation" (2 Nephi 4:30).

Since I have again put my trust in God, and not in my sore "arm of flesh," my burdens are lighter, my mind is clearer, and my joy is full.

THE LORD FORBID IT

One of the most profound and rewarding experiences that our family has had as we opened up the scriptures seeking direction and counsel began in June 2001. My husband and I were living in Montana, but we were not excited about our growth and development there. However, we were not sure where the Lord wanted us to go and what He wanted us to do.

One evening we opened up the Book of Mormon with the question, "Should we leave Montana?" We opened to 2 Nephi 3:19–21, where Gidgiddoni exclaims, "The Lord forbid it. . . . we will prepare ourselves in the center of our land." This struck us as our answer. We still weren't prepared to go. We hadn't learned the things we were supposed to. We decided to stay but to get out of our rut and set goals, goals for every aspect of our lives: physical, mental, spiritual, professional, employment, student, callings, family, and so on. If we focused on preparing ourselves here, Heavenly Father would prepare the place where we were to go.

What else were we to learn? One night at institute, it occurred to me that we had hardly read our scriptures together since we had been married! The bishopric had even challenged us all to read the Book of Mormon. We took this as a revelation that perhaps the preparation we were to do included studying together. In my prayer before my scripture study that night, I asked Heavenly Father to confirm in my reading that this was a true revelation. I opened up to my page marker at Doctrine and Covenants 17:1 and read, "Behold, I say unto you that ye must rely upon my word, which, if ye do with full purpose of heart, you shall have a view of the plates [or that which you desire to see!]." With this counsel in mind, my husband and I set out to prepare ourselves for greater growth by reading our scriptures as a family.

This family commitment of relying on the word by turning regularly to the scriptures brought increased help and direction from a loving Heavenly Father. Answers to questions about where to go to college, what to study, housing, and employment were all made clearer by opening the scriptures. Learning to trust in the Lord even though the pathway seemed dark and uncertain has allowed us to face other uncertainties in life with greater trust and faith in our loving Father in Heaven.

CALLED TO PREACH

The decision for a girl to serve a full-time mission can be one of the most important decisions she can make in her life. She doesn't deal with the same pressure to go that a boy at age nineteen may deal with, but she does deal with other issues. She may be in the middle of her college career, or she may have already completed her education and be working at a place that she really enjoys, or she may be actively dating, knowing that one of her main purposes in this life is to find an eternal companion and have children. There is, of course, always the fear of what others will think of her, the unreasonable thought that no one wants to marry a returned sister missionary, and so on. The list of reasons the adversary tells us not to serve a mission can be endless.

In August 2002, I was working as a massage therapist. I was twenty years old, and the thought of serving a mission continually crossed my mind. One particular day, in the middle of giving a massage, I felt a deep spiritual, peaceful feeling that the Lord wanted me to serve a mission. A few days later, I received an inspired letter from my parents telling me the many things that they both had learned from serving their missions. The following Sunday, I met with my bishop to pick up my mission papers. I was going to go serve the Lord.

As usual, when one makes a decision to follow the Lord, the adversary kicks in at full speed. Satan began to put thoughts into my mind that I wasn't strong enough to be a missionary—physically, spiritually, or emotionally. After three months of battling with the adversary, I gave in. He won. I decided that I would not serve a mission and that it had just been a crazy idea.

Three months later, I moved in order to continue my career as a massage therapist. I felt as though my career was just beginning. I had many job offers working at day spas, for chiropractors, or even for the school I had attended. I took on a few of these jobs and began building my clientele. Still, an unsettling feeling was upon me. It seemed that no matter which direction I turned in life, I couldn't get rid of this feeling.

Between November 2002 and May 2003, I received many spiritual promptings that something in my life needed to change. One prompting was a phone call from my mother. Out of the blue, she said, "If you are worried about the finances of a mission, we will help support you." Another one was in a blessing that I received from my older brother. In the blessing, he said, "Your Heavenly Father knows the thoughts and intents of your heart."

These promptings, along with a few others, led me to rethink serving a mission. This time, though, I knew I had to make up my mind and that I could not turn back on my decision. I began to pray and ask for direction and guidance. I also prayed specifically to Heavenly Father, explaining that if He wanted me to serve a mission, I expected a direct answer from Him—one strong enough that I could turn back to for strength when times got tough.

The first weekend in May, I drove home to watch my younger brother in his high school play. When I arrived, I pulled my mom and dad aside and asked them to fast with me, so I might receive an answer about serving a mission. After sacrament meeting finished, I walked out into the foyer and there was my home stake president. I began small talk with him, asking him how his son was doing on his mission. After we talked for a bit, President Smith turned to me and asked, "When are you going to go on your mission?"

Of course, the tears began to flow as I felt that my prayer was beginning to be answered. President Smith must have sensed that I needed someone in whom to confide my fears, hopes, and dreams of serving a mission, so he set up a time to talk to me later that day. During our meeting, he shared with me his testimony of the gospel and his knowledge that God knows us as individuals. He said that if we want God to speak to us, then we read from the scriptures. He then gave me a blue copy of the Book of Mormon that had no markings in it.

As he handed it to me he said, "I know that if you have faith and say a prayer in your heart, that you will turn to the scripture that God wants you to read." Relying a lot on President Smith's faith and a little bit of my own, I opened the book. My eyes immediately went to Alma 42:31, which reads, "And now, O my son, ye are called of God to preach the word unto this people. And now, my son, go thy way, declare the word with truth and soberness, that thou mayest bring souls unto repentance, that the great plan of mercy may have claim upon them. And may God grant unto you even according to my words. Amen."

My prayer had been answered the way that Heavenly Father knew I needed to hear it.

Through this experience, I learned that Heavenly Father knows who I am and He knows my needs. He also knew that the only way I could serve a mission with 100 percent of my heart was to receive a profound, absolute answer. I'm grateful for a loving, patient Heavenly Father who never gives up on us, but who waits until we are spiritually ready to receive the promptings He has prepared for us.

THAT THEIR PRAYERS MAY BE ANSWERED

While I was visiting family in Salt Lake City, my granddaughter told me that she and her husband had been thinking about selling their beautiful home. This surprised me because they seemed so happy there. However, it turned out they had good reasons: they wanted to move closer to her and her husband's work, and one of their sons had been harassed for a long time by several cruel neighborhood boys. However, they didn't want to make a big mistake. There were also compelling reasons to stay where they were, including great teachers and lots of good neighbors and lifelong friends.

They had been praying for several months to know what was right for their family, and they knew they needed guidance from the Lord. One day my granddaughter was searching in the scriptures, hoping to have the book "fall open" and give her an answer, like she'd been told can happen. Her Book of Mormon literally did fall open to the last page of Mormon and her eyes went to the last verse on the page, Mormon 9:37: "And may the Lord Jesus Christ grant that their prayers may be answered according to their faith."

My granddaughter said she felt strongly that if she'd have faith in the Lord, their prayers would be answered. She wanted to know what I thought. I promised her I'd read it and ponder it myself when I returned to my son's home that night.

A strange thing happened. I went to bed very tired that night. I read a bit from the old, big Book of Mormon my son always placed by my bedside when I visited. I forgot all about what I had promised to do, and I went to sleep.

I woke early, and as I was lying in bed, waiting for sounds of the others in the household, I decided to read my scriptures for that day. I took the big book, let it fall open, and there was the last page of Mormon staring at me! It rather shocked me as I only then remembered what I had talked about with my granddaughter. I read it over and over. As I did, I realized how much it was helping me with my biggest worries! Right then I said a prayer for both of us—for all of us! It meant a lot to me and made me feel that I too need more faith and that answers can also come to me through reading my scriptures.

Because of this scripture, my granddaughter and her husband decided to put their home up for sale and leave it in the hands of the Lord. If it sold, they'd move. If it didn't, they'd stay. They are moving right now!

FEAR NOT TO DO GOOD

My husband and I had been faced with litigation from a competing business. Complaints against us made to different authorities, both local and state, started before we even opened our doors. We knew through fasting and prayer that our family was to make this move and start this business. It was not an easy endeavor but we put our faith in the Lord and made the plunge.

At first, we thought we just needed to be cooperative in the investigations and questionings, and that by doing this everything would be okay. After two and a half years of continuing complaints and threats, we were served with legal proceedings to be decided in a federal court. This caused us a tremendous amount of stress to say the least. We went to trial and prevailed. Surely this would be the end of it.

That was not to be, for the judgment was appealed, and there were more trials and hearings. We could either choose to defend ourselves or close our business. We had no other choice, but the stress and anxiety was terrific.

In the Salt Lake Temple one day, I came across Doctrine and Covenants 6:33–37. As I read these verses, I could feel the Spirit tell me that this was the answer to all my concerns.

Broken down, here were my answers:

Verse 33: "Fear not to do good." We were doing good; my husband and I both tried to serve the people of our community. "For whatsoever ye sow, that shall ye also reap; therefore, if ye sow good ye shall also reap good for your reward." The Lord was telling us to keep our chins up and continue doing what we knew to be right and everything would be okay.

Verse 34: "Therefore, fear not, little flock; do good; let earth and hell combine against you, for if ye are built upon my rock, they cannot prevail." At times it truly felt as though hell was coming against us. This verse gave us direct comfort that if we stood true to the faith and kept the commandments, the false accusations could not hold up.

Verse 35: "Behold, I do not condemn you; go your ways and sin no more." This verse gave us the comfort that we were not condemned but that we needed to show greater love and continue to work on forgiving the individual who was causing us so much grief. "Perform with soberness the work which I have commanded you." Here was the reinforcement we needed to continue in our business, as we had been inspired from the beginning.

Verse 36: "Look unto me in every thought; doubt not, fear not." Here again was the counsel that told us that Heavenly Father knew who we were and what we were faced with.

Verse 37: "Behold the wounds which pierced my side, and also the prints of the nails in my hands and feet." These precious words filled my heart with gratitude, knowing what Jesus Christ had done for us and all who would partake. These words helped me put into perspective that what we had gone through, or may be called to go through, was absolutely nothing compared to what our Savior went through for each of us. "Be faithful, keep my commandments, and ye shall inherit the kingdom of heaven. Amen." Here was the final loving counsel that gave us the strength to continue.

It has been almost five years since I found this scripture, and the persecution continues. These verses have brought such comfort. Many times, they have been the balm of Gilead to comfort my aching soul.

NEVERTHELESS

I asked God for a miracle—not only a miracle, but a miracle with a deadline. As the deadline grew nearer, it appeared as if my prayer was being answered. The solution offered seemed so obvious and convenient, and yet somehow I knew it wasn't my answer. It didn't make sense, but I didn't feel right about it. People who knew what I needed were shocked that I didn't accept this simple solution. One person went so far as to tell me that I blew it. My deadline was one month away, and I had turned down what appeared to be my miracle.

Two weeks passed, and my phone rang one evening. I was offered another answer to my prayer—unfortunately, it came at a higher price. The cost would be leaving my job and people I loved and traveling out of town to work. I put down the phone and picked up my Book of Mormon. I prayed for confirmation that this was indeed the answer to my prayers.

Time after time, I opened to verses that contained affirmation. The verses contained the words "go," "travel," "journey." Continually I prayed, asking if I should work out of town, and continually I received clear direction.

When the deadline arrived to say yes or no to giving up the job I loved, my boss and I discussed my future. He said it would be nice if we had a road map. I replied that although I didn't have a crystal ball, I did have a compass. That night, I prayed for direction again. I opened my scriptures—to a page of maps. I decided that Heavenly Father had a sense of humor. I also knew that He was telling me that I held the road map in my hands.

I prayed again and opened to Doctrine and Covenants 18:2: "Behold, I have manifested unto you, by my Spirit in many instances . . . wherefore you know that they are true." It was true. I knew I had been given the same answer many times.

Even though it was obviously the answer to my prayers, this was not what I wanted. I couldn't understand why I had to turn down the opportunity at my home job only to end up taking a job out of town. I knew it was what Heavenly Father wanted but I couldn't figure out why. I opened to Doctrine and Covenants 63:20: "Nevertheless, he that *endureth* in faith and doeth my will, the same shall overcome" (emphasis added). I had to exercise my faith and go.

The first day at my new job was a little nerve-racking. I was scared and sad. When I started my drive home, it was dark and cold. Suddenly a deer jumped on the road. Its face was at my window, and I looked it in the eye, yet somehow I didn't hit it. My heart was pounding, I was shaking, and it was the last straw.

I said aloud, "What am I doing here?" I longed to return to my old job. "I want to go home!" I called out. Suddenly I remembered that I was where Heavenly Father had led me.

I said one more thing aloud to the darkness, "Nevertheless!" Then, at that moment, I made a commitment to do the Lord's will, regardless of my own desires. I trusted Him. I trusted that because I was doing His will I would be blessed, just like the scriptures had promised.

From that moment on, blessings poured out during my travel for the new job. I was given temporal blessings, which is the miracle I had prayed for, but the spiritual blessings were beyond measure.

Heavenly Father knew I needed more than a job with benefits. I was blessed with my own Sacred Grove. As I traveled that road back and forth, I grew closer to Him than ever in my life. He spoke to me through snow-covered hills, silver-lined clouds, sunsets, and even a swaybacked horse. My heart swelled, and tears flowed often. My Heavenly Father knew me. He loved me. He wanted to teach me the things that would help me return to Him, and I was willing to learn.

Just when things seemed fine, my world got turned upside down again. Another job opportunity arose that would allow me to return to my original employer—this time with benefits. I thought about one of the scriptures I had opened to when contemplating the first job change. It referred to leaving "for a time."

Had the time passed? I knelt and prayed, then opened my Book of Mormon to Alma 1:26: "The people also left their labors to hear the word of God. And when the priest had imparted unto them the word of God they all returned again diligently unto their labors." I realized I had left my labors at home and the result was that I was able to hear the word of God in my travels. I knew Heavenly Father was telling me it was time for me to return again to my hometown job.

I am not a person who makes decisions easily. I question the decisions I make. I am often plagued with regret. However, these decisions did not cause me any regret because I let Heavenly Father guide me. I received His guidance because I opened the scriptures. They truly were my own road map, my compass. When I was willing to follow those directions with a simple "nevertheless," the real miracle was received.

Notes

1. Gordon B. Hinckley, "The Shepherds of Israel," *Ensign*, November 2003, 60.

Chapter 11

RESPONSIBILITY
TO CHURCH

The third area of responsibility we have, according to President Gordon B. Hinckley, is to the Lord and His work. I remember President Hinckley expounding on this several years ago when he used a pair of binoculars during a general priesthood meeting to explain magnifying one's priesthood and calling. That visual taught me a valuable lesson I have never forgotten. Though he was speaking to priesthood holders, I'm sure his counsel applies to all who serve in the Church. He said:

When you put the lenses to your eyes and focus them, you magnify and in effect bring closer all within your field of vision.

To every officer, to every teacher . . . there comes the sacred responsibility of magnifying that priesthood calling. Each of us is responsible for the welfare and the growth and development of others. We do not live only unto ourselves. If we are to magnify our callings, we cannot live only unto ourselves. As we serve with diligence, as we teach with faith and testimony, as we lift and strengthen and build convictions of righteousness in those whose lives we touch, we magnify our priesthood.[1]

What a blessing it is to have a Liahona to guide us in our responsibilities in the Lord's work.

COMMENDING THEMSELVES TO THE LORD

While serving in the Young Women organization, I was asked to accompany our youth to stake youth conference, held in a beautiful mountainous area about ninety minutes from our home. It turned out to be a frightening but growth-inducing experience.

The weekend was wonderful, but on the last day returning from a service project in another area, I got a flat tire. Many youth and leaders helped replace the flat tire with the "doughnut" from my trunk, but due to the rough roads, I had to travel slowly back to camp.

I had several concerns about getting home. I was afraid that the doughnut might go flat, because the roads were not only very rutty but covered with sharp rocks. I felt my only hope was to travel slowly. Also, the journey back to the highway included an unmarked turn, and I feared that if I were left behind by the others, I would not find the turn, especially in the dark.

Not only did those things concern me, but several bears had been sighted that weekend. We had been warned repeatedly of the danger the animals presented, so the idea of walking to the highway if I broke down was out of the question in my mind. Though I carried a cell phone, there was no reception.

As I prayed for assurance and pondered what to do, I turned to my Book of Mormon, which fell open to Ether 6:3–4, which read, "And thus the Lord caused stones to shine in darkness, to give light unto men, women, and children, that they might not cross the great waters in darkness. . . . [A]nd it came to pass that when they had done all these things [preparations] they got aboard of their vessels or barges, and set forth into the sea, commending themselves unto the Lord their God."

After reading those verses, I felt the Lord understood my concerns about losing my way in the darkness. I decided to leave a little before the rest of the group to try and get to the highway before the sun went down. I also knew that as I "commended myself unto the Lord," He would watch over and protect me on this journey.

As I read in Ether a little further, I was reminded that the Jaredites' journey was not an easy one, and I felt that it mattered not whether I got lost or got another flat tire, as long as I knew that the Lord was with me. I left with confidence that the Lord knew where I was, that He understood my concerns, and that He would take care of me, whatever the circumstances.

Well, I did miss the turnoff, and I did get another flat tire, but an inspired friend saw me go the wrong way and chose to follow me (half an hour out of his way) just in case I had more tire trouble, and he was able to rescue me. I was grateful that the Lord had blessed me through the scriptures to be able to find the direction and comfort I needed, and then to gently remind me, through my friend, of my constant need for a Savior.

The following day I received an e-mail from my missionary son in the South Pacific telling me that he was leaving on a small boat to serve on a distant island. Since my son was not a swimmer, my first response should have been fear, but I quickly recalled my scripture reading from the day before. Upon rereading that page in Ether, I felt confident that the Lord knew where my son was and that my son was not a good swimmer. I knew in my heart that "no monster of the sea would break or mar him" (Ether 6:10) in his travels. I knew that, just like the Jaredites, my son would be protected from the fury of the sea, and like his mom the day before, he would arrive safely. Like my scriptural counterparts, I shed tears of joy "because of the multitude of His tender mercies over [me]" (Ether 6:12), a simple youth leader/missionary mom.

LIGHT OF HIS COUNTENANCE

I was newly called to be in charge of planning the monthly Relief Society home, family, and personal enrichment meeting in my ward. Because it was a small ward, no sisters were available to give me assistance in coming up with ideas and planning meetings. I alone decided each month what the sisters should learn.

I was only twenty-four years old, and the majority of the sisters were quite a bit older and in other stages of their lives. Many of them had to travel thirty to sixty miles to attend this meeting, and I wanted to plan things that would make the trip worthwhile for them. It was hard to know what to do because I wasn't sure what they would be interested in. I created a survey to get feedback from the sisters, but not many of the sisters returned them to me.

As the date of the first enrichment meeting grew closer, I needed to make a decision and start planning. Being at a loss as to what to do, I knew I needed to turn to my Savior. I knew that He knew the needs of the sisters and could direct me. I decided to open my scriptures in search of guidance. I said a prayer for the Spirit to direct me to a topic for the meeting, and I opened the Book of Mormon.

The book opened to 3 Nephi 19:25, which read, "And it came to pass that Jesus blessed them as they did pray unto him; and his countenance did smile upon them, and the light of his countenance did shine upon them, and behold they were as white as the countenance and also the garments of Jesus; and behold the whiteness thereof did exceed all the whiteness, yea, even there could be nothing upon earth so white as the whiteness thereof."

Immediately, I felt impressed that I should focus on having the light of Christ in our countenances as a topic for the Enrichment meeting. I was able to proceed easily from there with the ideas flowing from the Spirit. For such a small problem, I'm grateful that the Lord was willing to direct me through the scriptures to know His will for His daughters.

OUR FIRST PARENTS

As I was sitting in the chapel at the temple during a youth baptismal temple trip, several thoughts went through my mind. While I understood the concept of being baptized for the dead, I felt I was lacking in my understanding of the importance of this ordinance. I knew what it was that we were doing, but I didn't feel too much significance about the family names I was doing. It seemed like a chore or obligation that had to be fulfilled.

So, while sitting there, I grabbed a copy of the Book of Mormon and opened it. I opened it to Helaman 5:6 and started reading. About one-third of the way into the verse it was talking about "our first parents who came out of the land of Jerusalem."

As I read, I realized why these baptisms were so important. The verses explained to me, in plenty of detail, that I needed to remember my ancestors, their works, and all the good that they did, so that I could follow their example. Verse 8 seemed to specifically address how important it was for me to do baptisms for the dead, not just for the ancestors' but for my own sake too. Verse 8 told me that I wasn't doing this service that I "may boast, but that [I] may do these things to lay up for [myself] a treasure in heaven, yea, which is eternal, and which fadeth not away; yea, that [I] may have that precious gift of eternal life, which we have reason to suppose hath been given to our fathers."

I learned that by doing both this vicarious baptismal service for my ancestors, and by studying their lives and their good deeds and then following their examples, I receive hope for eternal life. I appreciated what Helaman taught, so I could begin to comprehend the significance of what I was doing in the temple.

COME UNTO THIS PLACE

One Sunday after sacrament meeting, my husband and I were called into our bishop's office. As we got ourselves situated, our bishop calmly and confidently extended the call to me to be our ward Relief Society president.

My first thought was, "Surely he's mistaken. He has the wrong person in the office." As I asked him how he came to this decision, he explained that he and his counselors had a small list of potential sisters they were considering. After I had spoken in sacrament meeting that day, he felt prompted by the Spirit to extend the call. I felt deeply touched and moved by his response. However, I knew that I needed my own confirmation from the Lord. I could not accept this call without a personal witness.

I went home that Sunday afternoon and began to prayerfully petition the Lord. Almost immediately, I felt Satan's presence. All manner of doubt and fear filled my soul and mind. I continued to pray, and then I reached for my scriptures. What happened next will forever remain in my mind and ultimately gave me the strength and courage to accept the call.

I turned to the Doctrine and Covenants and read:

> Prepare ye the way of the Lord, make his paths straight . . . the gospel [shall] roll forth unto the ends of the earth, as the stone which is cut out of the mountain without hands shall roll forth, until it has filled the whole earth. Yea, a voice crying—Prepare ye the way of the Lord, prepare ye the supper of the Lamb, make ready for the Bridegroom. Pray unto the Lord, call upon his holy name, make known his wonderful works among the people. Call upon the Lord, that his kingdom may go forth upon the earth, that the inhabitants may receive it, and be prepared for the days to come, in the which the Son of Man shall come down in heaven, clothed in the brightness of his glory, to meet the kingdom of God which is set up on the earth. (D&C 65:1–5)

Then I read in Doctrine and Covenants 100:4–8:

> Therefore, I, the Lord, have suffered you to come unto this place; for thus it was expedient in me for the salvation of souls. Therefore, verily I say unto you, lift up your voices unto this people; speak the thoughts that I shall put into your hearts. . . . For it shall be given you in the very hour, yea, in the very moment, what ye shall say. But a commandment I give unto you, that ye shall declare whatsoever thing ye declare in my name, in solemnity of heart, in the spirit of meekness, in all things. And I give unto you this promise, that inasmuch as ye do this the Holy Ghost shall be shed forth in bearing record unto all things whatsoever ye shall say.

As I read these scriptures, a peace and calmness filled my mind and soul. I believed that the Lord had called me, through my bishop, to fulfill the calling to be Relief Society president and to be an instrument in His hands. I was called to help further His work; to prepare the way for His return; to share my testimony of my Savior and His gospel; to strengthen, edify, and assist through the guidance of the Spirit those sisters whose hearts were heavy, whose hands were hanging down and whose knees were feeble (see D&C 81:5), and to help the Lord bring back His children who walked in darkness. I was counseled to not rely on my own strength; I was to rely on the Spirit. I wanted to serve the Lord, and I knew it was His desire for me to help Him.

As I fulfilled my calling, the Spirit did impress upon my mind the thoughts and words that I should speak. When things became difficult in my calling, I turned to these scriptures for comfort, peace, and reassurance that I was meant to "come unto this place."

HARDEN NOT YOUR HEART

I was in my third year of teaching early morning seminary. The first two years had been enjoyable, but this class seemed different. Many of them did not want to be there. They did not like seminary, and I felt they did not like me. I knew I could be a good teacher, but these students seemed to want me to fail. They seemed to see me as the enemy. If I succeeded, they failed. If they could get me to fail, they had succeeded. At least, that is how it appeared to me.

Despite the different approaches I tried during the year, I felt I was not succeeding at all. I was very discouraged. I made class rules to modify their poor behavior in class. I seated talkative students away from other talkative students. Nothing worked. All I succeeded in doing was making the young people dislike me—and seminary—even more. As time went on, I could tell that my frustration was causing me to lose the Spirit. I began to dislike the "problem students."

One day, as I was pleading with Heavenly Father to help me gain control of the classroom and endure to the end of the year, I felt impressed to open the Book of Mormon to find an answer. I randomly opened the book and found myself in Alma 12:10. As I read, I came across many references to being hard-hearted.

Was that the counsel I needed? I continued reading and found four more references in verses 34–36 counseling "harden not your heart." By now, I was pretty sure what Heavenly Father was trying to tell me. I had been determined to make the class behave. I wanted to have things my way. I had not been sensitive to the needs of my students. I had not been teachable or humble. My pride was hurt, and I had wanted to retaliate.

As I read on into Alma 13, I found more such references. In all, I found counsel regarding hard hearts twelve times in the verses I read. It was obvious to me what the Lord was saying. I needed to back off, show love for my students, and not be so headstrong about making the students change to suit my idea of the perfect classroom.

It was a real eye-opener for me. I needed to be meek, submissive, loving, kind, and teachable. I have never had scripture hit me as hard as it did on that occasion.

SERVE

Because my husband's patriarchal blessing mentions many times that he will be involved in worldwide missionary work, we had saved our money and looked forward to going on missions as soon as our youngest child was well established and on her own. When that time arrived, we prayed to know the will of the Lord, and if the time was right to put in papers for a mission.

We were surprised that we did not get a good feeling about serving. We continued to pray and even fasted for guidance. We finally came to the decision that it was not yet time for us to go. So we revamped our plans and decided to stay in our home, and my husband continued in his profession.

But this left me a bit up in the air. The one thing that we had been steadily headed toward was now on hold, and I was uncertain what direction I should take. My children were grown. I did not work outside the home.

Years earlier, I had become involved in family history work and had enjoyed it. But, busy with raising children, I eventually put that activity aside. Now I wondered if I should begin again.

As I sat in the temple one day waiting for the session to begin, I asked the Lord to give me direction about what I should be working on now. I opened the scriptures to 3 Nephi 27:21 and read, "Ye know the things that ye must do in my church."

Then I felt a little foolish. Of course! I shouldn't wait to be commanded in all things. The Lord has made it abundantly clear that we should all be researching our family roots and getting our ancestors' temple work done. I appreciated that direct answer.

A month later, my husband was called to serve in the stake presidency. We were told it could be a ten-year calling. So this was why we were not to put in papers for a mission!

This unexpected turn of events made my husband's path very clear; he knew what he would be doing. But what was I supposed to be doing for the next ten years? I needed more guidance. Having raised a large family, I was used to being busy and involved. I knew the Lord had plans for me, and I wanted to find out what those plans were.

Again, I petitioned the Lord and again opened the Book of Mormon. I opened to Mosiah 4:14 and began reading, and the entire plan was spelled out for me. Mosiah 4:14-15 told me to continue to serve and teach my adult children. Verses 16 through 26 instructed me to serve and help the poor and needy. Verse 27 cautioned me that it was all to be done in wisdom and order.

Now I have a plan that will carry me into the future, over the next ten years if need be. I will serve my family, the poor and needy, and my deceased ancestors. I have my answer. I know my direction.

NOT REQUISITE TO RUN FASTER

I had been filling the calling of ward camp director for our Young Women organization for about six years. For most of those years, only one of my daughters was old enough to attend camp with me. But this was the year both of my daughters were old enough to go, and I was excited to have that experience. I knew they would have fun because camp is always fun!

About a month before we were to go to camp, I received a call from a member of the stake presidency asking if I could meet with him. During that meeting, I was asked to be stake camp director.

I was torn by this calling. I knew that with each new calling came specific blessings, and the experiences from these callings were immeasurable. However, I also knew our ward had a hard time finding camp directors, and this year was no exception. I was sure to be the only adult sister going. I was putting the finishing touches on our camp preparation. Besides, I truly wanted to go to camp with my daughters. I wanted to see my younger daughter experience camp for the first time, see her expressions and her excitement. Was that such a wrong thing to want?

For the first time in my adult life, I didn't accept a new calling right away. Instead, I told the counselor in the stake presidency that I would get back to them after I had prayed about it.

I went home, talked to my husband, prayed, and thought about all the pros and cons. Then I remembered the counsel of our stake presidency, that you can find your answers in the scriptures if you will only open them. I opened my scriptures randomly and found myself at Mosiah 4:27: "And see that all these things are done in wisdom and order; for it is not requisite that a man should run faster than he has strength. And again, it is expedient that he should be diligent, that thereby he might win the prize; therefore, all things must be done in order."

I decided that to accept the calling as stake camp director would have been extremely hectic on such a short notice, and it would have made me run faster than I had strength. I counseled with the member of the stake presidency, and after explaining my situation, he agreed. I went to camp as a ward camp director and had a wonderful year. The sister who served as stake camp director did a great job, and I enjoyed being with my daughters.

MY PEACE I GIVE UNTO YOU

I had been asked to play a piano solo in church on Mother's Day. I love playing the piano, and I love sharing my talents, but I have a terrible fear of playing in front of large groups of people. My hands shake so much that I can't play steadily. My nervousness takes all the feeling out of my usual passionate playing, and I never feel like my performance goes well.

But I had previously agreed to play and was now sitting in sacrament meeting, just minutes before it was my turn, and I was already shaking nervously. I wanted this to be special for my mom. I wanted to do a good job. Mostly I wanted to be calm, so I could do my best and bring a spirit of peace to the meeting. I opened my scriptures in an attempt to find comfort, and I was pleasantly surprised at the scripture I opened to: John 14:27, which read, "Peace I leave with you, my peace I give unto you: not as the world giveth, give I unto you. Let not your heart be troubled, neither let it be afraid."

I knew this scripture wasn't talking about playing the piano, but the peace that came flooding over me as I read the comforting words, "my peace I give unto you" and "let not your heart be troubled, neither let it be afraid" comforted me. I immediately felt peace rush over me. I was physically comforted as my hands stopped shaking, and I was spiritually comforted to know that Heavenly Father cared enough about me to send me His spirit through this simple verse at a time when I needed to feel His love.

IN THE PATH OF THEIR DUTY

As an elder serving on a small island, I often used the Liahona Principle. My companion was disobedient. The members struggled to understand and live the gospel. Our mission president was far away. I felt greatly alone, and I yearned for the Lord's companionship. As I turned to the Lord, I found reassurance and guidance. I also found myself constantly being told to not judge, and to be patient and humble.

One day, as I was pondering how I should overcome judging the people and my companion, I opened my scriptures to see what guidance I could receive. "Lord, what wouldst Thou have me know?" was the question I had in my heart. The answer? "I would that ye should behold that the more part of them are in the path of their duty, and they do walk circumspectly before God, and they do observe to keep his commandments and statutes and his judgments according to the law of Moses" (Helaman 15:5).

They were doing the best they could with the best they had. What more could they do? I needed to not judge them for what they did and accept them as they were.

I learned that opening the scriptures is like saying, "Lord, what is Thy will, that I too might have that same purpose?" As a result, the Lord blessed me during my time of service on that island. As I continued to seek the Lord's guidance by opening the scriptures on a regular basis, I was uplifted and directed. Never have I felt such closeness with the Holy Ghost as I did then. I learned of the Lord's absolute guidance in His work by turning to the scriptures.

Notes

1. Gordon B. Hinckley, "Magnify Your Calling," *Ensign*, May 1989, 46.

Chapter 12
RESPONSIBILITY TO SELF

The fourth responsibility President Gordon B. Hinckley says we have is to self. He told priesthood leaders that in addition to rest, exercise, a little recreation, and going to the temple, "[you] must have time to study. Every church officer needs to read the scriptures. He needs time to ponder and meditate and think by himself."[1]

During those quiet times of study and reflection, we often learn our most important lessons. We all have various obstacles to overcome, some much greater than others. President Hinckley has also said, "Few of us do not have at least one Goliath to contend with. . . . There is not a person in this Church who needs to succumb to any of these forces. You are a child of God. You have His power within you to sustain you. You have the right to call upon God to protect you."[2]

Our scriptures are one of the greatest gifts God has given us to guide us in our efforts to improve ourselves. Whether we have major personal Goliaths or smaller, routine, day-to-day obstacles to overcome, direction, understanding, and help is only a Liahona away.

HAVING YOUR GARMENTS SPOTLESS

Seven years had passed since I had been to the temple. During that time I had fallen away from the Church. I guess "fallen away" is not the best phrase to use. It wasn't as if it happened to me involuntarily. I made one small bad choice, which led to another. Before I knew it, my bad choices began to outweigh my good choices. Unfortunately, as the frequency increased, so did the severity.

After I joined the Church, I believed in the iron rod. Now I had not only let go of it, but I had also taken a step away. As in Alma 36:16, "I was racked, even with the pains of a damned soul." My sins had caused so much pain and damage, I didn't know if I could ever overcome them. I was ashamed, miserable, and full of sorrow. The most painful thing was the loss of the companionship of the Holy Ghost. How had I let myself lose all the blessings I had gained?

I felt like such a failure that I felt unworthy to even try getting back on the right track. What right did I have to go to church on Sunday, when I had sinned while knowing better?

I took many years to come back to the Church with complete commitment, to take the sacrament again, and to have the Holy Ghost with me. The temple seemed so far away, yet it called to me. It was that longing that finally brought me to full repentance.

I knew I could never return to where I belonged without the final step of going to the temple. Finally, I received my recommend again, and Alma 36:20 became my favorite scripture, because I was living it. "And oh, what joy, and what marvelous light I did behold; yea, my soul was filled with joy as exceeding as was my pain!"

As I held my scriptures with temple recommend in hand, two questions lay in my heart: "Am I really worthy to hold this recommend? Do I belong in the house of God?" I opened the Book of Mormon.

Alma 7:25 was the first verse I read. "And may the Lord bless you, and keep your garments spotless, that you at last may be brought to sit with . . . the holy prophets . . . having your garments spotless . . . in the kingdom of heaven to go no more out." I could renew my temple covenants and be made spotless again. I could remain worthy and never let go of the iron rod again. I could keep the Holy Ghost with me.

"And my soul doth exceedingly rejoice, because of the exceeding diligence and heed which you have given unto my word" (Alma 7:26). My Heavenly Father was happy that I had finally turned to the Book of Mormon and applied its teachings in my life.

"And now, may the peace of God rest upon you . . . according to your faith and good works, from this time forth and forever" (Alma 7:27). I had longed for peace for so long. If there was one thing I had learned, it was that there was no peace to be found in sin. Now I knew I could find peace and keep it forever if I kept my covenants and lived my faith. Even when things in my life get hard, there is One who will give me peace always.

As I knelt there, I was overcome with the reality of the Atonement of Christ. I always believed Christ had died for the sins of the world, even before I joined the Church, but suddenly I knew that He died for *my* sins. "There could be nothing so exquisite and so bitter as were my pains. . . . [O]n the other hand, there can be nothing so exquisite and sweet as was my joy" (Alma 36:21). I knew with all my heart Christ had paid the price for the pains I had caused myself, and my heart was filled with joy.

There was one final issue to face. My husband was out of state when I finally received my recommend. He was struggling to overcome his own pains and was not active in the Church. I was worried about how he would feel. When I told him of my accomplishments over the phone, he was somewhat hurt and discouraged. He felt like I was leaving him behind, moving forward without him. The night before I went to the temple for the first time, I was thinking about his reaction. I opened my scriptures for guidance. They fell open to Doctrine and Covenants 25:9, which read, "And thou needest not fear, for thy husband shall support thee in the church." What peace that gave me!

Early the next morning, my husband called to tell me to enjoy my day at the temple. My testimony was strengthened. I knew through answers given to me in the scriptures that I belonged in the temple and that Heavenly Father, knowing all the desires of my heart, wanted to bless me with peace of mind. I will never find that kind of peace in the world, but it is always waiting for me in the scriptures.

TENDER MERCIES OF THE LORD

I was raised in a good home with loving parents who provided well for me. Although my father was an atheist and my mother an inactive member of the LDS church, I was baptized at eight years of age.

Today, memories are vague and details sketchy about my childhood, but someone familiar to me—someone that I, as a child, was supposed to be able to trust—started taking advantage of me sexually. At every opportune moment, he used me in this manner. Family get-togethers became a much-dreaded experience for me. I remember hiding in fields, an empty lot, old sheds, a ditch, and even trees and haystacks.

Eventually this man made me feel as though it was all my fault. He reinforced fabricated stories and made threats, and I felt too guilty to tell anyone.

As a result of this experience, I learned to not trust people, and I remember feeling confused and dirty about the human body. As a teen, I slipped into drug and alcohol use. I learned early on how to mix and dose several substances to create a desired effect; I'd found the "answer" to the void in my life. I lived this way a few years, believing I had everything under control—despite the fact that I overdosed, wrecked cars, sold drugs, had friends who were dying, spent a lot of money, and hurt my family terribly.

Finally, I became careless. I was arrested one night and faced several charges, narrowly escaping rehab. Believing I could keep my dependencies in check without the any type of help, I attempted to get it together. I started college. Soon I began having a relationship with a man. My skills in my chosen profession were advanced, and I had the opportunity to attend a major university, all expenses paid by a private benefactor.

As I was considering this offer, I found out that I was pregnant. I was devastated once again, not only for the turn of events but also because I could hardly bear the thought that all my drug-using and drinking may have already affected my unborn baby. Irrationally, I began wondering what I was going to do with a baby anyway. I wasn't ready to be a mom! And I certainly didn't want to marry! Going with this feeling, I scheduled an abortion. This was the turning point in my life.

The next few days were agonizing. A voice in the back of my mind kept telling me over and over not to follow through with this. The day finally came. Although I had no idea what else I was going to do, I dialed the doctor and cancelled the appointment. Immediate relief set in, but I simply lay down and cried. How long I lay there I do not know—but something stirred within my heart. I remember this well. With purpose, I decided to pray.

As I knelt, I was enveloped with a new determination such as I had never before felt. Unsure that I'd be heard, I pleaded with Heavenly Father to help me to overcome the substances that had plagued my body for so long and to grant me the strength to become a good mother. In return, I promised that I would become an active member of the Church and do everything in my power to nurture this child and raise him or her to be familiar with the gospel of Jesus Christ. As I arose from this prayer, I felt immense relief. I had no idea how to accomplish what seemed so impossible. I was literally "living on a prayer."

Then another wonderful thing happened. One morning I received a phone call. On the other end of the line was a cheerful voice that claimed to be my visiting teacher (what's a visiting teacher?). She and another sister came to my house the next day. It was a short but meaningful visit, and because of the scriptural references they'd left me with, my interest soared. Acting on this momentary excitement, I rummaged through a box until I found an old, beat-up copy of the Book of Mormon.

As I opened its cover, I came across a passage that jumped out at me. "The tender mercies of the Lord are over all those whom he hath chosen, because of their faith, to make them mighty even unto the power of deliverance" (1 Nephi 1:20). At this point, I realized how deeply I yearned for peace in my life. I wanted to change for me and my baby. I started feeling sorrow for my own personal shortcomings. I felt heavy.

I kept reading and came across Alma 22:16, yet another passage that stood out. "If thou desirest this thing, if thou wilt bow down before God, yea, If thou wilt repent of all thy sins, and will bow down before God, and call on his name in faith, believing that ye shall receive, then shalt thou receive the hope which thou desirest."

Could there actually be hope for me? My desire at that moment was to know Heavenly Father was real, that He was listening to me, that He did indeed love me. Again, I knelt in prayer. This time I was resolute and seeking forgiveness. Incredible peace and warmth like I had never before known confirmed to me in these moments that I was at long last on the right path. I had found the missing piece to my life's puzzle.

Over the next few weeks, I changed dramatically. Substance withdrawal is painful, and to couple it with a pregnancy and abandoning "friends"—well, I thought I'd die before I finally made it to a tolerable level. I know I had help because there's no possible way I could have suddenly given up so much and pulled through it alone. I wasn't alone. As time passed, I continued my study of the Book of Mormon. I was so mesmerized by the trials, faith, and testimonies of an ancient people.

Several years have gone by, and I am blessed with a wonderful husband and children, sweet friends in the Church, and all the comforts honest, hard work can bring. How can I ever express in words the gratitude I feel for having listened to the Spirit and desired change? Life for me would have been very different had I not listened.

I can never deny this wonderful book, the Book of Mormon. The truths and lessons it contains have sculpted my life and instilled in me an impenetrable belief in the gospel and the plan of salvation.

Over the years, I have been able to heal a bit at a time from my former life. It has taken the help of priesthood blessings, prayer, and a consistent daily search for the answer—whatever the question may be—through the scriptures. I can attest to the fact that much can be overcome in this life through fasting, prayer, and a sincere desire for change to take place.

HE CANNOT BE SLAIN

No single experience has done more to challenge and strengthen my faith than one I had in the spring of 2005.

My wife and I attended a class at which a nutritionist commented that all of us have cancer cells in our bodies and, depending on the quality of our nutrition, those cancer cells will either be able to take over our bodies, or our bodies will be able to fight off the cancerous cells. That was it. It was a short comment that came in passing, but it had a tremendous impact on me. It wouldn't leave my mind.

About three weeks later, I noticed a slight throbbing in a certain part of my body. For some reason, my mind immediately grabbed hold of the idea that I probably (I skipped right over *possibly*) had cancer. My mind locked in on this idea, and I could think of nothing else. I started losing sleep. My appetite shrunk to almost nothing. I was filled with dread and discouragement.

I reminded myself that out of the hundreds of relatives in my very extensive family, none had ever had cancer. That idea didn't ease the dread and fear of what might happen to me. Then I did some research and found out that the particular cancer I was afraid of was exceptionally rare. These facts did not ease my fear.

Finally, after receiving various promptings, I opened the Book of Mormon looking for answers; I opened to Alma 18:3. This verse talks of how Ammon could not be slain. As my wife and I discussed it, I concluded that I was being taught that I would not be slain by this affliction.

So what should I do? I opened the Book of Mormon again to see what I must do to overcome this supposed affliction. I opened to 3 Nephi 19:16. Here, Christ is commanding the people to kneel down and pray to Him. I took this as an answer that I must turn to the Lord in prayer.

After opening the scriptures, I felt enlightened and uplifted. Over the next couple of days, I felt much better, but it didn't last. I looked up medical information a few days later, and the fear, dread, and terror returned. I felt such great anxiety that I could think of nothing else.

For most people, the logical answer would have been to go to the doctor. This wouldn't work for me, however, because I knew that even if the doctor told me I didn't have cancer, the fear wouldn't go away. I would wonder if the doctor missed it or made a mistake. My real problem was not cancer, it was fear—fear of what would happen to my family if I died—and I needed to know how to deal with that.

During this time I found a general conference talk given by Elder Richard G. Scott concerning faith and fear ("Trust in the Lord," *Ensign*, November 1995, 16). In this talk, Elder Scott taught that until we get to the point of saying, "Thy will be done" when praying to the Lord in the midst of a trial, we are not able to fully draw down the powers of heaven to bless our lives. This struck me because I had never felt so engulfed in utter dread and terror. I knew that I needed all the blessings the Savior could bestow upon me; however, I felt too scared to pray that the Lord's will would be done. I was worried that His will would result in my death.

Finally, in a quiet moment, I knelt down. With a trembling heart, I prayed that the Lord's will would be done. I felt so nervous; I almost felt that I was giving the Lord permission to take my life right then and there. I was so worried about who would take care of my wife and my soon-to-be-born daughter.

I would like to say that upon uttering this prayer my discomfort, terror, dread, and fear vanished and I was left to bask in peace and joy. It was not like that. I felt fine physically, yet the mental games were almost more then I could bear. I was trying to replace my fear with faith and I was praying that the Lord's will would be done, but I didn't know how to feel okay with whatever the Lord's will would be. Saying "Thy will be done" and wholeheartedly meaning those words was proving to be more then I could handle.

Throughout this difficulty, I kept turning to the Book of Mormon. Over and over the verses I turned to kept telling me to repent. I knew that I needed to repent of this extreme lack of mental and emotional faith, but I didn't know how.

Finally, I read in Doctrine and Covenants 19:27, "Look not for a Messiah to come who has already come." The lesson was obvious. I had already been told what to do. If I was to be saved from this mental affliction, it would be by prayer, repentance, and the tender mercies of the Lord. I had to start thinking of others and their needs. I had to discontinue activities that wasted me mentally, and I had to stop doing things that would cause me to recall my fears.

What I have finally begun to learn is that the Lord will not lie to us. Indeed the answers from the scriptures that I received from the beginning have been the answers that I needed to overcome my fears.

THOU SHALT CONCEIVE
AND BEAR A SON

I have struggled with infertility for eighteen years. I have had one child myself, and I know her birth was a miracle that came about because of much fasting and prayer. We have also experienced two wonderful adoptions—a daughter and a son. We were preparing to check into adoption options for a third time, and I began to wonder if it were possible to have the next child myself. Was there any way? Though I had prayed and fasted for many years on this subject, I intensified my efforts. My question to the Lord was, "If we adopt again, where should we begin? And if I could have the next child myself, how can my body be healed or changed to make that possible?"

I also had a second, less-important subject I was praying about: How could I develop self-control in my eating habits? I seemed to have plenty of ambition to eat better when my stomach was full, but I lost that ambition the next time I was hungry. The result was a frustration with myself and a slow, constant increase in my weight. I often begged the Lord to help me find the self-control to eat the way I knew I should.

In early September, I fasted twice. Four days after my second fast, I received the most powerful answer I have ever experienced. I had not read my scriptures for several days and had determined not to go to bed without reading my scriptures. I was currently reading in the Book of Mormon, but when I was ready for bed that night, I couldn't find my scriptures. I grabbed an old Bible off the bookshelf and opened it to read. What I read changed my life!

The scriptures opened to Judges 13. The woman in the chapter, Manoah's wife, is barren. The angel of the Lord came to her and told her to "drink not wine nor strong drink, and eat not any unclean thing: For, lo, thou shalt conceive and bear a son" (Judges 13:4-5). The entire chapter emphasizes this concept, and the truth of the answer pierced my heart. I was to eat no unclean thing, and I would bear a son.

I knew the promise was given to me just as it had been to Manoah's wife centuries ago. This was not only a method with which I could prepare my body to bear a child, it also gave me a powerful reason to have self-control in my eating. My eating habits changed immediately. In three months, I was pregnant. We were so excited. Little did I know I was only beginning my journey.

Christmas came. I was pregnant now. Did I have to worry so much about eating perfectly? Over the holidays, I did not eat as well as I had been, and I miscarried! I went into the bedroom and opened up the scriptures; they opened up to Doctrine and Covenants section 82. The entire first half of the section was my answer.

In my journal, I wrote, "The Lord says I ask for a revelation and don't follow it. He is not bound if I don't do my part. . . . I feel like my Heavenly Father is lovingly teaching me a very important lesson about exactness in following His principles. . . . It's a hard one to learn."

I began to wonder if I could really do this. I prayed to better know what food was unclean for me, but I didn't receive any clear answers. I flipped the scriptures open again. They opened to Doctrine and Covenants 58:26, where I read, "It is not meet that I should command in all things."

I needed to decide myself what my goals were and then stick with them. So, again, I made up my mind about what I could eat. I knew that the main thing I needed to learn was trust in the Lord and His timetable.

The extra effort of self-control and obedience has brought a joy and peace into my life that is hard to describe—it is wonderful. Yet time races on, and I am now over forty years old. To me, trusting in the Lord means that even though this journey is much longer than I had hoped it would be, I know He keeps His promises. I have no doubt the promised blessing of a child will come, but right now it's the journey that is so rewarding!

THE MORE RIGHTEOUS

A lovely Latter-day Saint lady whose husband returned home to heaven too soon told me one Sunday she hated the word "endure." She said she was sick of enduring life by herself. She asked herself, "What's the use of enduring alone?"

Of course, I listened and tried to encourage and comfort her. I know personally how hard life can be. It's long and difficult and can wear a person out. I have wondered myself if it is worth all the effort to endure by trying to keep the commandments, follow the prophets, and live as our Savior wants. It can seem beyond our capabilities at times.

One day I received an answer to that question while reading in 3 Nephi 10. This part of 3 Nephi records the destruction of all the wicked following the Savior's death. As I was reading, I wondered if I would have been among the few remaining survivors. I have needed repentance more than I care to remember, and I have plenty of weaknesses that seem to rule me from time to time. So, as I read I thought the question, "Would I have survived?"

Reading on, I came to verse 12, and there was my answer. "And it was the more righteous part of the people who were saved, and it was they who received the prophets and stoned them not."

I thought, "I am one of the more righteous—not the most righteous—but more righteous. Like them, I have received the prophets. It is worth it to endure," and a beautiful, quiet peace came over me—certainly a gift from the Holy Ghost.

Latter-day Saints can chart their course by choosing to follow the prophets, the commandments, and the Savior. When we make this choice, albeit imperfectly but with faith and trust in Heavenly Father, we are ensured eternal life with Him. What could be better?

POWER OF THE WORD

There was a time when my testimony of the truthfulness of the restored gospel was shaken. I had decided I would not read the

Book of Mormon for a while, but rather, I would continue my daily scripture studies by reading the Bible. I would hold fast to the one thing I knew for sure—God exists. He hears my prayers, and He loves me. Through reading the Bible and praying daily, I continued to feel peace, experience the joy of raising a family, and feel God's influence in my life.

A month had gone by, and it was time to do my visiting teaching. Suddenly, I realized what a void had been created in my life by not reading the Book of Mormon and feasting upon the words of God. Although I don't recall the exact scripture that was included in the visiting teaching message that month because so many years have passed, I do remember my feelings as I read the scripture. My soul flooded with great joy as the Holy Ghost witnessed to me the truthfulness of the Book of Mormon. I was unable to hold back the tears.

What a welcome feeling! Now I more deeply appreciate this second witness of Jesus Christ; I realize what a blessing it is to have the privilege of feasting upon it daily. The Book of Mormon has brought more light, hope, wisdom, and understanding to all aspects of my life. It also reminded me of the things I need to do to repent, so I can have the privilege of returning to the presence of our loving Heavenly Father and enjoying all He has in store for me eternally.

Just as one who doesn't realize how thirsty he is until he takes a drink of water, I hadn't realized how much I had been missing. I think every person who diligently reads the Book of Mormon could write his own record of how certain verses of scripture cause their soul to expand and to sing songs of redeeming love (see Alma 5:9). There never has been a time when reading the Book of Mormon has not benefited me in some way, whether I read only one verse or an entire chapter. I love how this book has delivered me out of Satan's influence and helped me overcome bad habits simply by the power of the word (see Alma 5:5). It has illuminated my soul by the light of the everlasting word (see Alma 5:7). With the additional light of the Book of Mormon, I can more clearly see God's plan for me.

LITTLE IMPERFECTIONS

One particular incident of opening the scriptures has had a profound effect on me. I had been doing much soul-searching and was trying hard to repent of my sins. I was gaining a much better understanding of the Atonement and its significance, and was starting to feel so much better about myself and that I was a beloved daughter of God, when I started to notice that I was going over and over everything I thought I might have done wrong in my entire life. I couldn't get these things off my mind. Some things were extremely minor and some things much more serious.

I went to the Book of Mormon and it opened to 2 Nephi 4:15-21, where Nephi writes about the things of his soul. I read and reread those verses and felt the Savior's love but still could not get the problems out of my mind. I prayed about it and still had the feeling that my answer was in those verses, but I just wasn't getting it. A few days later, I read the verses again and got the same answer, so this time I prayed about what I was doing wrong. The answer came to me very clearly.

Because I do not understand many of the phrases in the Book of Mormon, I had been using a reference book. I had the profound feeling that was where I needed to go to find the answer, so I could understand those verses and what they meant for me. What a wonderful answer I got.

The author said verses 15-35 are known as the Psalm of Nephi. Here Nephi rejoices in the scriptures and the things of the Lord, while at the same time expressing concern for his mortal frailties and shortcomings. He questions why someone as righteous as Nephi would be so concerned. He notes that perhaps the answer is found in the fact that the more righteous people become, the more "little imperfections" glare at them in the light of truth. Things bother them now that hardly registered in their minds before. He observes that such people should rejoice that they are noticing such things in their lives, because it is a witness that they are well along on the path back to God. He said that the rejoicing is possible because of the Atonement.

There was my answer. A wonderful feeling of warmth and peace flooded over me and tears flowed. What I had desired most was happening.

TITLE OF LIBERTY

Here I go again. I woke up to another "dumb" dream, but I knew it wasn't dumb. I was trying to throw an oversize football through a basketball hoop but failed miserably in comparison to my friend. His throw was long and beautiful, a perfect spiral. Mine only went a few feet.

It was only another dream reminding me of a problem I had recognized for a long time—that of comparing myself to others. Sometimes I saw myself as being better than others, which I knew was also a problem, but usually I found myself not being good enough, at least good enough in relation to what I thought others thought about me.

This dream reminded me again that I still had a long way to go with this frustrating struggle in my life. "Heavenly Father," I prayed, "if there is anything in my scripture reading this morning that will help me with this problem, please help me recognize what it is."

I opened to my bookmark in the Book of Mormon and started reading Alma 46. Through cunning devices and flattering words, Amalickiah had led away many of the Nephites. "Those are the same techniques that Satan uses on me," I thought, "to get me to compare myself to others. But how do I deal with that?"

Moroni gave me my answer and told me what I needed to focus on to be free (Alma 46:12-13):

"In memory of [my] God, [my] religion, and freedom, and [my] peace, [my wife], and [my] children—and he fastened it upon the end of a pole. [These are the things I needed to focus on, rather than the words or expectations of others.]

"And he fastened on his head-plate, and his breastplate, and his shields, and girded on his armor about his loins; and he took the pole, which had on the end thereof his rent coat, (and he called it the title of liberty) and he bowed himself to the earth, and he prayed mightily unto his God for the blessings of liberty to rest upon his brethren."

Spiritual armor to protect my head (thoughts) and heart (feelings) and mighty prayer for blessings of liberty are the tools I needed to free me from comparing myself to others—my personal title of liberty, something I could hoist upon my bedroom mirror and view as a daily reminder of whose side I am on and whom I am striving to serve.

WHOM THE LORD LOVETH, HE CHASTENETH

Toward the end of my sophomore year of high school, I dated a guy for a couple months before I had the courage to get out of the situation. Nothing terribly bad ever happened—I never even kissed him—but when thinking about the situation I always felt guilty. Many times I had prayed and asked for forgiveness, but this feeling lasted into the next year. I finally came to the point where I couldn't handle it anymore. I felt guilty for something that had happened months before, yet I had changed my ways. I wanted to be happy again to feel that peace that only comes from being worthy of the Spirit. I wanted Christ in my life fully again.

So one day I fasted and went to do baptisms in the temple with faith that I would receive confirmation about whether I had been forgiven. As I sat down in the temple, I picked up a Bible and decided to turn to my favorite passage, Proverbs 3:5–6. I continued reading through verse 12, when I was deeply touched by the fact that the reason God chastises and corrects us is because He loves us.

"My son, despise not the chastening of the Lord; neither be weary of his correction; For whom the Lord loveth he correcteth; even as a father the son in whom he delighteth."

I looked down at one of the footnotes, which cross-referenced Helaman 15:3. That verse reaffirmed the same point: "he chasteneth them because he loveth them," and I felt good about it. I went to the footnote again and was led to Hebrews 12:5, where I read, "Despise not thou the chastening of the Lord, nor faint when thou are rebuked of him: For whom the Lord loveth he chasteneth."

It was like my life story captured in the scriptures. I couldn't believe it. It repeated everything I had been going through and then everything I needed to hear. It was such a good feeling.

As I thought through everything I had just read, I realized this was my answer! Tears ran down my cheeks as I felt Heavenly Father's love surround me as I sat in His holy house. I felt so loved by Him that He would let me have an experience like this. Knowing I finally had put forth effort and found an answer was such a comfort to me and made me so happy. I couldn't stop smiling, and I wanted to jump up and shout for joy! I'm forgiven! I felt so good inside. It was a peace I had waited for, for so long, and it felt so good to finally have it. There was a real change in my countenance. Real happiness and pure joy shone through for the first time in months.

I couldn't stop smiling! I was so happy. I had made an honest mistake that any human could make, but I had since done what I knew to be right. I had asked for forgiveness, fasted, prayed, and gone to the temple. Most important, I had a sincere desire to be forgiven and to change my life. I put the Atonement into action, and I was forgiven, and there is no better feeling in the world!

AS I SAID CONCERNING FAITH

(The following story is written by a nonmember of the Church. The missionary who tracted Sara out and taught her in England asked her to share her story, and this was her reply.)

I was skeptical to say the least. You told me to close my eyes, open the Book of Mormon, and there would be my answer.

My whole problem revolved around faith. I believed there may be something, a greater force, whatever, not necessarily a man. So I closed my eyes late one evening in the quietness of my bedroom and let the book drop open. My eyes were drawn to verse 6 straight away, like there was nothing else written on the pages; the verse was in Alma 15. "And it came to pass that Alma said unto him, taking him by the hand; Believest thou in the power of Christ unto salvation?"

To be honest, I thought it was a lucky hit, so I closed the book and opened it again. This time, the book opened to Alma 37:36: "Yea, and cry unto God for all thy support; yea, let all thy doings be unto the Lord, and whithersoever thou goest let it be in the Lord; yea, let all thy thoughts be directed unto the Lord; yea, let the affections of thy heart be placed upon the Lord forever."

When I next saw you, you asked me how things had gone. I told you about the verses I had read, and it was like someone had switched on a light in your eyes. You were thrilled. We sat and had a discussion about faith, and I asked, "how you can have faith in something that you can't see?" I went to bed that night praying to Heavenly Father for a sign of His existence. I was still skeptical. This went on most nights with no sign, or if there was one, I missed it.

About five days later, I opened the Book of Mormon again. This time, the book opened to Alma 32:21: "And now as I said concerning faith—faith is not to have a perfect knowledge of things; therefore if ye have faith ye hope for things which are not seen, which are true."

To this day I will use the Book of Mormon when things seem to be against me and my brain is so mixed up. I feel it's like having a guardian to guide you when you are struggling. What amazed me was there was no way I could have known any of these verses because I had only started reading the Book of Mormon.

Notes

1. Gordon B. Hinckley, "Rejoicing in the Privilege to Serve," June 2003 Worldwide Leadership Broadcast, 22.
2. Gordon B. Hinckley, "Overpowering the Goliaths in Our Lives," *Ensign*, January 2002, 2.

Chapter 13

A LIFE-CHANGING
PRINCIPLE

The Liahona Principle is a true principle. I have seen it used thousands of times. My personal life has been blessed immensely as I have looked into my Liahona and found direction, understanding concerning the ways of the Lord, help in solving my personal problems.

My family's life has been blessed greatly the same way. My callings in the Church have given me the opportunity to know hundreds of people who have applied this principle and received direction and enlightenment from Heavenly Father. It is a life-changing principle when applied with faith. Lehi and his family are not the only ones who have been blessed with a compass to show them the direction they should go. Each of us has direct and easy access to our own personal compass. We simply have to open the scriptures.

As you reach the end of this book, I hope that you have a better appreciation of how Lehi's compass worked according to the faith, diligence, and obedience they gave to it. I hope that you also better understand that they were slothful to obey its directions and, as a result, tarried in the wilderness, did not travel a direct course, and suffered on their journey. But Lehi and his family still arrived at the promised land! They were not perfect in using the compass they had been given, but they did use it, and they eventually reached their destination.

What a great parallel for us. "For just as surely as this director did bring our fathers, by following its course, to the promised land, shall the words of Christ, if we follow their course, carry us beyond this vale of sorrow into a far better land of promise" (Alma 37:45).

The words of Christ contain the answers to all of our problems. His words are most loudly heard in the scriptures and through living prophets. As we open those sacred books with faith, we will always find direction and understanding concerning the ways of the Lord, and help in solving problems. We can learn where we are really at and what we need to do. We can receive a second or a third witness to things we have already heard or felt. We can find that the way is easy, that Heavenly Father will enlighten us more than we previously realized, and that the process is wonderful.

All we need to do is have a sincere question or thought in mind, open our scriptures, and apply what we read to what we are thinking about. Most of the time, the answer will be surprisingly clear. Sometimes it will offer an easy solution, sometimes a very difficult one. Occasionally, we may not understand or recognize the answer. However, with patience and faith, and as we continue to seek direction, understanding will come. As we give heed to the compass we have been given, we will follow a more direct course in our journey and prosper in that area of our lives.

Write down your Liahona experiences. The direction, understanding, and help you gain is something you will want to remember to help you stay the course and progress in your journey. It is much easier to give heed to the compass if we can go back and read and be reminded of the instruction we received.

I hope the insights you have gained from the thoughts and stories in this book have been uplifting and enlightening to you, inspiring you in the use of your scriptures. Without a doubt, the most life-changing and meaningful story you read will be the one that you write in the pages of your own heart—your own personal experiences with the Liahona Principle.

ABOUT THE AUTHOR

Bradley R. Wilde was born and raised in Welling, Alberta, Canada, and has spent his career as a health care professional in Worland, Wyoming. He has served in two stake presidencies, as a counselor in a mission presidency, as a bishop, and in a variety of other Church callings.

Bradley is the author of *It Pays to Understand the Book of Mormon*, a children's workbook; and *I Make Me Sick*, a book about how thoughts and feelings affect the body.

He and his wife, Debi, are the parents of seven children.

Bradley would love to hear how the *Liahona Principle* has blessed your life. Please e-mail your experience to him at drwilde@ liahonaprinciple.com, or mail it to 100 TaBi Drive, Worland, Wyoming, 82401. For further information, go to his his website at www.liahonaprinciple.com).